Book-Collecting as a Hobby

Book-Collecting

as a Hobby

In a Series of LETTERS to EVERYMAN

by P. H. MUIR

ALFRED · A · KNOPF

NEW YORK · 1947

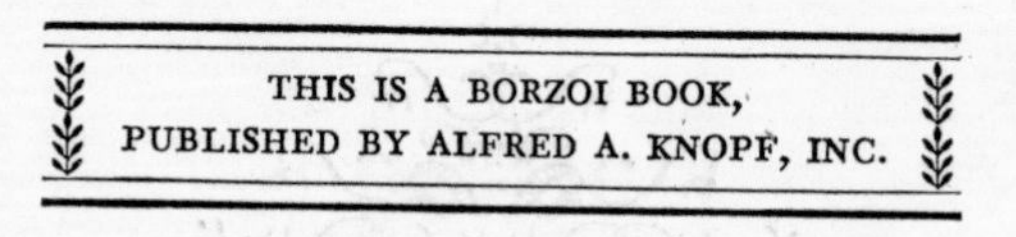
THIS IS A BORZOI BOOK,
PUBLISHED BY ALFRED A. KNOPF, INC.

FIRST AMERICAN EDITION

Contents

Illustrations

(*follow page 38*)

Illustrations

facing page

Book-Collecting as a Hobby

LETTER ONE

How to Begin

DEAR EVERYMAN:

YOU are interested in books and you have bought a good many in your time, but you would not call yourself a book-collector. You think that there is some fundamental difference between mere book-buying and book-collecting, and you want to know what that difference is. In a way you are right, for although all book-collectors are book-buyers, not all book-buyers are book-collectors. You have bought this book because you want to know the answer, and my idea in writing it is to try to provide one. You may wonder why some fifty thousand words are necessary to do this, and you may suspect that this means that book-collecting is too difficult and expensive for plain, ordinary folk to be bothered with. If that is your idea, I hope you will read a little further, because it is precisely the possibility of such a mistaken view that has prompted me to write this book.

Book-collecting is not exclusively a hobby for rich and leisured people. It is less a matter of money than of method. I know many people of quite modest means who have gathered valuable and important collections with no greater expenditure than casual book-buying might entail. I hope to show you how it is done and how you too, if you are so inclined, may enrich your shelves and your experience by becoming a book-collector.

Even the rarest of books cannot be commanded simply by the possession of a long purse. Crœsus may collect first editions of Shakespeare, but some of these exist only in one or two fragments, all of which are in public libraries. The Folger Library at Washington has a magnificent collection of Shakespeare, one of the finest in the world; but there are many gaps in it. So that even for Crœsus it is not simply a question of ordering whatever he feels inclined to pay for. There is much for which he would be only too willing to pay if it could be found. He must, however, combine patience with a readiness to buy whenever the opportunity offers itself, and the same principle applies in more modest realms of book-collecting.

First of all, then, what you require is a plan. However casual your book-buying has been in the past, you will almost certainly find, if you look through your shelves, that it shows tendencies in certain definite directions. If you arrange your books roughly under subjects, you will surely find that some subjects loom larger than others, and this, of course, will show where your own personal interests lie. There you have a possible basis for collecting.

If it turns out that emphasis lies, shall we say, on Shakespeare, you must think again. There is hope for you if it lies on something more accessible.

Later in this book I will suggest some collecting paths that have not been over-explored (see Letter II), but I should like to make it clear from the start that this is going to be your collection and you must decide its basis. You must choose the subject and decide its limits and its form.

You may think that an obvious remark. Of course, you will be thinking, If you are going to collect the books, they will be books of your own choice. What else would you be likely to collect? Believe me, the danger is a very real one. You may, quite unsuspectingly, find yourself led away into collecting what somebody else thinks is a good author or a suitable subject, and you may find yourself expounding the courage of other people's convictions rather than your own.

There is, in fact, a great deal of fashion in book-collecting. You will not need reminding of the fickleness of fashion, nor will you forget that to be in the fashion, whether in clothes, holiday-making, or book-collecting, is bound to be an expensive business. And I don't want your book-collecting to be an expensive hobby; quite the contrary. Therefore, if A is an author whose work you find particularly attractive, do not be deterred from collecting him by the fact that B, the famous critic, or C, a friend whose opinions you respect, has compared A's work very unfavorably with that of D, a better-known or more fashionable author. Stick to your guns. A is the man you like; then by all means collect him and leave D to those who genuinely enjoy his work or who prefer to be in the fashion rather than to strike out on their own. It is not your business as a collector to back favorites for the posterity stakes, although I will not deny the probability that you will spot a very promising dark horse. Let me illustrate what I mean.

I spoke just now of collecting Shakespeare – the greatest of English authors – and I made it clear that, as a subject for the first-edition collector he is out of the question. If literary excellence were the only criterion he would be at the top of every collector's list; for even those of us who do not read poetry with pleasure may agree with Samuel Butler that Shakespeare's poetry is almost as good as prose.

At the other end of the scale are the dime novels that you probably read in your childhood as I did. Neither you nor I will pretend that these are literature. They are pure hackwork, ground out to a mass-produced pattern, beneath the notice of most literary critics, although you may remember an entertaining essay on them in *Horizon* written by George Orwell. Nevertheless, despite their lack of literary elegance, they entertained you and me as well as millions of others belonging to generations both older and younger than our own. And, say what you like about them, they filled a gap. Before we had graduated to Literature with a capital L, they fostered our interest in reading and kept it alive when it might have flagged and possibly have died without them. Moreover, they have a very special place in social history, for many of the ideas uppermost in the minds of small boys may be traced directly to their fondness for this kind of book, and the boy is still the father of the man. I do not wish to overemphasize their importance, but merely to indicate that they might well form the subject of a very interesting collection. They would be difficult to find—thus providing all the fun of the chase, which is an important part of the sport of book-collecting—and they should not be expensive to buy. Michael Sadleir, Montague Summers, and other investigators have written learned and fascinating treatises on the early counterparts of these books—the popular fiction of the eighteenth and nineteenth centuries. There is a chance for some like-minded collector to do the same for cheap literature of the twentieth century. But I am not suggesting it should be you: I am merely illustrating the twin facts that a collection need not necessarily consist of good books, and that all the fun of the fair may be had at very little expense.

Between the two extremes mentioned in the last two paragraphs are all kinds of possibilities of contrast and almost limitless opportunities for the exercise of individual choice in collecting, including many fascinating bypaths that have never been explored at all. Choose, then, one of these rather than a well-beaten track; you will get much more enjoyment out of it, you will be a pioneer, and, most important of all, your pocket will benefit enormously.

Having chosen your subject or author, the next thing to do is to find out all you can about it. Suppose, for example, you are very interested in detective fiction and that you decide to make that the subject of your collection. You will, I hope, collect first editions of the books. That raises a technical point that you may think of as one of the stumbling-blocks if you are a complete beginner. How can you tell whether a book is a first edition or not? The fact that first editions appear to be so much more valuable than later editions seems to you to presuppose that there is some magical difference that constitutes a first edition

— a difference detectable only after a long course of study for which you have neither the time nor the inclination.

I shall have a great deal to say about this in Letter III, and I will not pretend that it is altogether a simple matter. Much learning and great scholarship have been devoted to deciding problems of this nature. Some of the most important problems are still unsolved. No one can say to this day with any certainty what constitutes a first edition of Goethe's *Faust* or Voltaire's *Candide*, for example. Nevertheless, it is frequently true that any book is a first edition that does not contain evidence to the contrary. This is true of ninety out of every hundred books *that you are likely to collect until you are much more deeply involved in the subject than you are now*. It may easily happen that you never run across a problem of this kind in the whole course of your collecting career, though, for your sake, I hope that you will, and you yourself will welcome the solving of such problems as you progress. But you may forget all about it to begin with; so let us get on with the literature of detective fiction.

I would recommend you to start with John Carter's entertaining and excellently documented booklet on the subject, published by Constable at two shillings, and to follow that up with *Murder for Pleasure*, by Howard Haycraft (Appleton-Century, $3.00). This will give you tips for future reading. You will remember that Wilkie Collins and Edgar Allan Poe wrote detective stories, and there is the immortal Sherlock Holmes to consider. Lists and descriptions of the first editions of all these have been published and you will need to consult them. You will soon find other sources to consult, such as prefaces by E. M. Wrong, Dorothy Sayers, and others to collections of detective stories that they have edited, and you will begin to accumulate quite a reference library on the subject.

About reference books, however, you should go very slowly to begin with. They are of unequal value and they are apt to be expensive. It is a good plan always to borrow a reference book from a library if you can before buying it for your own shelves. When you have read and examined the book carefully, you can decide whether it is likely to be so indispensable for your purpose as to warrant your buying a copy for yourself. Good reference books are the best investment a collector can make; bad ones are a continual pain in the neck.

You are by no means ready yet to start buying books for the collection. The more slowly and carefully you start, the fewer steps you will find it necessary to retrace. The latter is a painful and expensive process and to be avoided as far as possible. You will make mistakes; we all do, even the most expert of us. They are unavoidable, but there are many that you can spare yourself by careful preparation. I suppose that you have a limited amount of money to spend on your collection, and there is the danger that, even if you don't buy one or two wrong books, you may spend far too great a proportion of your available cash on filling up your shelves with the common run of books, and when a rarity comes your way, you may not have the money to spare to pay for it. The common books you may pick up at leisure; rarities must be seized whenever they occur, for you may not see them again for a long time, and by then the price may have risen against you.

Before you buy a single book, therefore, try to make up your mind what are the important books in such a collection. Do a little scouting. Ask one or two booksellers about these important books, how recently and how frequently they have had them, what they are likely to cost. You will find that booksellers rather enjoy discussions of this kind and they will prove very helpful in sketching your plan of campaign.

We will suppose, then, that you have taken these first steps: that you have committed yourself to a subject and a plan and that you are now setting off on the hunt for actual books. You will do well to cultivate certain frames of mind in this book-hunting business, and although they are rather nebulous, very individual and personal, and will be infinitely varied according to the person who displays them, it may not be entirely useless for a very old hand like myself to attempt to suggest some of the secrets of successful book-buying.

I referred just now to a very prevalent idea among collectors that their selections are not of an age but for all time. It is a very natural weakness, and one that we all share to some extent. It is the feeling that your guess about what is likely to prove immortal in current literature is as good as the next man's. Whether you are right or not lies in the lap of the future, and none of us is likely to be there to see. It will do no harm if you are wrong in your guess, and may do good to preserve for posterity something that might otherwise have perished.

In the long perspective of that standpoint, such a notion is at worst harmless. It is only in the short view, and if it is allowed to become perverted, as I have so often seen happen, that it may not merely be harmful, but actually do much to spoil the rather fine flavor that book-collecting ought to have.

I mean that you should try to reckon the value of your collection rather in terms of the pleasure you will derive from it than in terms of its rising cash value. Do not be always thinking what your collection would be worth if you turned it into cash tomorrow. That way lies trouble. Do not misunderstand me. The collective value of a library will usually increase beyond the sum of the individual prices you have paid for the books in it, and the proportion of increase will rise steeply as the collection grows in size and importance. My friend Maurice Buxton Forman tries to secure for his library every edition of Keats's poems ever published anywhere. In consequence he has numerous editions that he knows to be valued only in shillings, or even in pence; but their value in a comprehensive collection of that kind is proportionately much greater than when they are found on the ten-cent shelf—if such a delectable hunting-ground still exists in these days.

Take it another way. Suppose someone set out to collect one book published every year from 1641 to 1941. (I will tell you in my next letter why I chose these dates; there is a reason for it.) The collector I visualize here would not be interested in the books from a reading point of view, but purely from the point of view of book-production. Therefore he would be sure, as far as possible, that the get-up of each book was typical of the period in which it was printed, and he need not care two cents about its literary content. He might very well find himself at the end of it with a collection of three hundred or so books not one of which was worth, individually, much more than he paid for it. All the same, if he had made his collection wisely and carefully, its value as a collection would be very many times the total cost of the books in it. As a library of reference in the history of publishing styles it would be invaluable and he would have conferred a great benefit on students of the subject by gathering it together. I shall have more to say on this subject in my next letter.

Another thing: such a collector might be very glad to pay far more than its intrinsic value for a book that filled an important gap in his dates, or one that was especially typical of a period. He would know, from practical experience, how very rare books of that particular date must be (and they would not necessarily be always the earlier books). How could he reasonably expect anybody less well informed than himself to value that book, out of its context, at anything like the value it has for himself?

Do you see what this is driving at? Do not harbor the illusion that you will be able, at any time, to turn your books over at a large profit. Such turnovers have happened quite frequently in book-collecting history. There was an example, and a very notable one, quite recently, when John Burns's collection of Sir Thomas More was sold, and realized prices far higher than he paid. There were exceptions. Some of the books sold for less than he gave for them. In my opinion this was probably not an error of judgment on the part of John Burns. He knew what he was doing, for he knew more about the rarity of Sir Thomas More's first editions than any other man of his time, he was a careful buyer, and if he paid what appears in sales-room judgment to have been an unduly high price, it was almost certainly because he knew how rare the book was and that the alternative might be between buying that copy and none at all. Moreover, the rise in value of Burns's collection came after many years, and it was partly the result of a specialized collection.

Nevertheless, if you view your books constantly from the angle of their probable cash value, you will deprive yourself of a great deal of the pleasure they ought to afford you. You will constantly have your ear to the ground for changes in fashion and price, you will be constantly wondering whether you are working on the right lines or whether you might not easily have chosen a more profitable one. The worst that can happen to you is that circumstances may compel you to abandon collecting, or you may need the cash or the shelf-space to start a new collection when the interest of the old one seems exhausted. Don't be cast down if you don't make a profit when you sell. The very collecting of the books, watching the collection grow, the glee and excitement when an obstinate gap has been filled – *these* things are the rewards of collecting, and unless you think about it in this way, you had better abandon the idea of becoming a book-collector and find some other and more remunerative hobby like fretwork or dog-breeding.

If cash values and capital appreciation are to be thought of at all, let it be as an afterthought; and the paradoxical nature of things is such that they will probably be added to you for good measure. But the more you seek them, the more completely they are likely to elude you.

One more thought on this side of the question and I have done with it for the moment. It will turn up again in Letter V, but we shall be much further on our book-collecting travels by then and I shall discuss it in a new light. My other momentary point about frames of mind is: don't be an incessant bargain-hunter. That, too, defeats its own purpose. Always be prepared to pay a fair price for a book that you need. You will get bargains, many of them, and they will become more frequent as your knowledge of your subject grows, especially if, as I hope, you choose an out-of-the-way one. But the booksellers, good fellows though most of them are, sell books for a living, and it is their business to know the value of their wares. They will not, generally speaking, grudge you a bargain here and there. Many of them will be the first to congratulate you if you find one on their own shelves, but they naturally do not approve of the man who only wants bargains. Why should they? Book-selling is their bread and butter.

The persistent bargain-hunter is only slightly less unpopular than the persistent bargainer. When you have become a regular customer, nearly every bookseller will do his best to meet you occasionally if you find the price of a book higher than you think it ought to be or than you can afford to pay. But don't make a habit of it. There *are* book-buyers for whom prices are specially marked up—the bookseller puts on a little more than he is prepared to take off. He knows he will not get the marked price from that particular customer, and he makes his plans accordingly. It is a hateful business, and I should not like to think that you might get on a black list of that kind. For there is such a list—not printed and circulated, but when booksellers get together and gossip (and no one enjoys this entertaining practice more than your good bookseller), there are smiles when certain buyers are named. Their curious habits are universally known—and catered for. Finally, if there is an alternative customer for a book, do you think the bargainer gets the first offer of it? I think you can answer that one for yourself. As I say, bargain-hunting and penny-pinching tactics defeat their own end – you may actually pay more in the long run.

Well, your first lesson is now at an end. You are armed and equipped to go forth and take a practical part in the Battle of Books. Good hunting, and in my next letter I will enlarge further on possible subjects that may interest you.

YOURS SINCERELY,

P. H. MUIR

LETTER TWO

What Shall I Collect?

DEAR EVERYMAN:

THIS chapter heading is a little misleading. I do not wish to lead you along paths of my own selection; I merely wish to rough out a few general ideas to show you samples of subjects that have not been overdone by other collectors and, by developing the lines along which these might be followed, to show the general plan of campaign in making a collection of this kind. It is, in other words, the manner rather than the matter of this letter that is important for you. So if I seem to presume that it is your collection I am writing about, you will see what I mean. I am just explaining what you would do if you were collecting any of the subjects I shall introduce to your notice.

You may not know that there is a whole book on the subject. It is called *New Paths in Book Collecting*.

The book is written by a collection of English and

American experts, each of whom writes one chapter on a special subject. The first chapter shows you how to begin and complete a collection of the work of a single author. The author chosen is Emily Dickinson, the American poet. She did not publish a single book during her lifetime, but after she died two friends arranged the publication of three very small volumes of her poems. This does not sound like a collection that would occupy anyone for very long, but read John Winterich on the subject in the first chapter of this book and you will see what fascinating prospects are open to a collector in even such a limited field as this. Emily Dickinson has an English counterpart in Manley Hopkins, who also published no books during his lifetime, but you would find it difficult to make a complete collection of his work.

The second chapter in *New Paths* is on detective fiction and has been published separately. Then follows a chapter with the rather curious title of "Ignoring the Flag." This suggests than an interesting collection could be made of books by famous authors which were first published in countries other than their own and gives numerous examples of books of this kind. Most of this chapter is concerned with English books which were first published in America and vice versa. If this interests you, you should take a look at I. R. Brussel's two books on *Anglo-American First Editions.*

C. B. Oldman, of the British Museum, writes a chapter on collecting first editions of music and gives an excellent list of books for further reading. He shows how little this field has been explored even now, and I shall presently have something to say about a particular kind of music-collecting.

There are chapters on collecting "yellow-backs" (the cheap bookstall fiction of Victorian times) and on war books. The final chapter is one of the most provocative and suggestive of all. It expounds the possibilities of collecting fiction in serial form, gives a list of famous books that were first published as serials, with the names and dates of the periodicals in which they appeared, and discovers all kinds of interesting reasons for collecting these rather than—or as well as—the first appearance in book form.

I will not enter at any greater length on the subjects in *New Paths*. If you are interested you will find details in each chapter of the book. But I rather like the idea that I briefly discussed towards the end of Letter I, of a collection to show the history of changes in book-production. I promised to give reasons why the dates chosen were 1641–1941. Well, first of all they make a nice round figure of three centuries. They give a feeling of breadth of scope and interest that would keep one busy for a long time. But why choose 1641 as a starting-point?

The reason is a rather interesting one and concerns a very important period in publishing history. This history, as far as it concerns printed books, begins, in England, with the year 1477, when William Caxton published the first book ever printed there. From that date until 1640 hardly more than thirty thousand books were printed in England. They are called "Short-Title-Catalogue" books because there is a list of them published under that name by the Bibliographical Society in London. This includes reprints of earlier editions; all the various editions of the Bible and separate parts of it, and pamphlets, Acts of Parliament, and other public records are counted each as a separate book. That is a very small number of books to appear in just over one hundred and fifty years. In the year 1943 with stringent paper-rationing in force, the number of titles published in a single year was nearly seven thousand. That will enable you to grasp how very few books were published in the early years of printing in England.

Printing was severely controlled not only by the Star Chamber, but also by the printers themselves, who were very anxious that the trade should not become overcrowded. The Star Chamber rigidly controlled not only what was allowed to be printed, but also, together with the Stationers' Company, the number of printers who were allowed to operate. There was no such thing as setting up in any trade that happened to take your fancy or for which you thought you had an aptitude. You had to secure a position as a freeman of the company or guild governing that trade. In this case it was the Stationers' Company. These tendencies restricted the number of printers and therefore the number of books printed.

In 1640 the trouble between Charles I and Parliament came to a head, and hosts of pamphlets—licensed and unlicensed—began to pour off printing presses, legal and illegal.

You have heard of "underground" printing presses run by revolutionaries in Russia and by patriots in occupied Europe and even in Nazi Germany. The same sort of activity was going on in England in the seventeenth century. A great revolutionary movement was growing and its champions exploited all the methods that revolutionaries always use. One of the most important of these is the illegal use of the printing press, and the reason for its use is to convert a sufficient number of people to the new ideas so that they may become the law of the land.

In 1644 Milton published his famous defense of the freedom of the press, in which he included the immortal passage beginning: "As good, almost, kill a man as kill a good book."

The immediate point to be made is that this spate of printing at once transformed the position, and it is much more difficult to attempt to record the total of printed matter after 1640 than it was before. Conversely, the number of books for our hypothetical collector to choose from is much larger, and he can select books representative of their period in style without having to pay fancy prices for them. Before 1640 almost any kind of triviality has some value; after 1640 there are masses of books and pamphlets of no literary or collecting value, purchasable almost for a few pence, which are, typographically speaking, truly representative of their time. That is a generalization which is not entirely true, but it is true enough for our immediate purpose.

In my previous letter I suggested collecting one book for each year of the period. Actually it would be very difficult to limit the selection to one each year and, as his enthusiasm grew, the collector would find good reason for enlarging its scope to the limits of possible expenditure.

Let us consider a few points bearing on this. A page of prose is set up in quite a different style from a page of poetry. Technical books, text-books, illustrated books, and chap-books each have conventions of their own. And there are the changing methods of binding to consider.

Then there is the question, which arises acutely about

half-way through the period, of books printed at private presses, also of new type designs and the revival of interest in fine printing for its own sake that occurred all over Europe in the eighteenth century, the influence of which was felt in England, too. The century was one of great inventiveness and craftsmanship in all directions. If you know anything at all about printing, you will have heard of a type called Caslon, which is in common use today. It was designed by an eighteenth-century type-founder named William Caslon, who issued his first sheet of specimen types in 1734. The collection might seek to include the first book printed in this famous type, and also to identify the first use of other famous types.

Baskerville is another type named after a great printer of this century, who designed his first type in 1750 and sent his first specimen sheet to Dodsley, the famous publisher and friend of so many authors of the period, in 1752.

John Bell, one of the founders of the *Morning Post* (others were Tattersall, founder of "Tattersall's," and Christie, the auctioneer), greatly influenced the designing of books. You will have heard of old books as having "f's" for "s's"; John Bell was the first to abandon the old-fashioned long "s," which he did in an edition of Shakespeare that he sponsored in 1785. There is an obvious book for our collection.

This was not the first time the short "s" had been used. Ames, in his *Typographical Antiquities*, published in 1749, abandoned the long "s" throughout the book, but this was a personal whim and had no general influence at all, whereas Bell printed a declaration on the subject and pointed out the advantages of abandoning the old practice.

Ames's book you might like to have anyway, because it will give you valuable tips in your search for representative styles. It is not inexpensive, but it is well worth buying if you can afford it. But I would still say that, for the abandonment of the long "s," Bell's 1785 Shakespeare is the book to have.

There are other famous printers in this period, like the firm of Foulis in Glasgow, and later on there are people like Bensley and Bulmer in the nineteenth century whose fine work is still underestimated, but who would come into this collection.

Invention plays a large part in modern printing, and it is only in very recent years that printing methods differ very largely from those of the ancients. I will mention one example of the sort of thing our collector would seek on these lines. You know what the word *stereotyped* means – something set in a fixed mold, or unchangeable. In origin it is a printing term. It means taking a mold from the metal type in which a book is set up so that the type can be broken up. If at any time it is required to reprint the book a new setting can be made by pouring molten metal into the molds. Thus you see the origin of the word. Type is movable and can be changed. Stereotypes cannot. The process of stereotyping, very much on the lines that printers still use it, was invented by William Ged, an Edinburgh goldsmith, and the first book printed from stereotyped plates was an edition of Sallust that he published at Edinburgh in 1739. It is a cheap little book that you may easily pick up on a stall for a quarter or less, for it is a Latin text; but it is an important landmark in the history of printing, although the practice did not come into general use until more than fifty years later.

Then there are the illustrators and the changing methods of producing book illustrations—the copperplates of the seventeenth and eighteenth centuries, the wood-engravings of Crawhall and Bewick—all these cut by hand on metal or wood by the artist himself. Then in the 1860's you have a change of method. Wood-engravings were still used, but the artist did not cut the blocks himself. A class of professional wood-engravers arose—the Dalziel brothers were the most famous—and the artist either submitted a drawing on paper which the wood-engraver copied, or he sometimes drew the design on the wood-block itself, but he very rarely cut the block; this was done by the engraver.

In 1800 the German Senefelder took out the first patent for lithography in England. This was first used for printing music and then for book illustrations, but it has been enormously developed until whole books are printed entirely by a development of the lithographic process, so the collection should include as early a specimen of lithography as can be found.

Mechanical reproduction of illustrations dates from the invention of photography in the second quarter of the nineteenth century. It does not much matter to our collector whether Daguerre, Niepce, or Talbot was the inventor of photography. The invention burst upon the world from at least two different quarters, and in the year 1839 at least two inventors laid claim to the invention of electrotyping, which is a mechanical method of producing a book illustration which is still in use today. In which book half-tone illustrations were first used I cannot say, but the half-tone block itself—that is to say, the block from which book-illustrations are produced on shiny paper, called "art" paper—probably goes back to the 1870's. Earlier color-printing methods were invented by Le Blon, George Baxter, Frederick Evans, and others.

Then there is binding to consider. The binding is certainly a most important part of a book, and style has varied and developed considerably during the period we are reviewing. Our collector would need specimens of eighteenth-century wrappers and boards, with all kinds of attractive marblings, and at least a sprinkling of calf, even if he did not aspire to morocco, which he might think less representative of England than of France in the eighteenth century.

Thanks to the researches of Sadleir, Carter, and others we know a great deal about publishing history in the nineteenth century. There is still much to be learned, however, and there are at least as many branches and sidepaths in the nineteenth as there are in the eighteenth century. The first book printed from machine-set type (nearly all books are now set by machinery) is an American handbook of sports and pastimes published in the 1880's. There were earlier attempts at mechanical composition in England. The *Family Herald* was set by this process in 1841–2, and so were some books. But the original invention was a failure. The first book of which an edition was bound in cloth by a publisher would be essential to our collection. The first cloth book has not been identified with certainty, but it was probably published by the firm of Pickering, its date is probably 1825, and it may be an edition of the *Works* of Dr. Johnson. If our collector could push that date back by even so much as a single year, he would confer a great benefit on trade historians.

The first book published with gilt lettering on the spine is known with some certainty. It is the third volume of a small edition of the *Works* of Lord Byron, in seventeen volumes, published by John Murray in 1832. The first two volumes of the set have the lettering on paper labels, which are pasted to the shelf-back of the volumes, but in the third volume the gold printing is made direct on to the cloth of the binding itself.[1] The book was bound by the firm of Leighton, and Archibald Leighton was the inventor of the process. The firm still exists and is one of the leading commercial binders of today.

My pen has already run away with itself on this subject and I must not spare it any more space, for there are other suggestions to be made for your consideration. But it is no bad thing to have enlarged so widely on one subject. It will show you how the modest notion of collecting three hundred books could be expanded until the field of operations became almost unlimited. If you are a young man looking for a hobby to last you for the rest of a very long life I hardly think you need look any further.

Either as a branch of the foregoing collection or as an entirely separate and self-contained subject, the collecting of music title-pages is worth very serious consideration. I do not mean that music should be dismembered and only the title-page preserved. That would be barbarism. I merely mean that the collection should be made with more of an eye on the publisher than his publication.

If you look at Kidson's *British Music Publishers*, issued in 1900, you will see how little is actually known about the history of some English music-publishers. One of the most important was John Walsh, Handel's publisher, and al-

[1] One set is known in which this occurs on the second volume.

though Kidson gives more than twelve pages to him—more space than to any other publisher in the book—he can tell us little or nothing about him or about his career and publishing methods. It is impossible, in the present state of our knowledge, to compile and date anything like a complete list of his publications, although Professor Deutsch is now at work on this very subject at Cambridge. Kidson also supplied most of the biographies of British music-publishers in Grove's *Dictionary*, to which he also contributed a most suggestive article on "Music Printing" with a list of books for further reading.

In an American book-collector's quarterly called the *Colophon*, Part 15, there is an article on Thomas Moore's *Irish Melodies* that throws some light on the Power brothers, who published them, and on music-publishing practice at that time. It also shows the importance of music title-pages.

These title-pages are rarely dated, but some publishers gave them serial numbers and it is sometimes possible to reconstruct a publisher's history by listing these serial numbers and comparing them with the known dates of publication of some of the music. The collector of music title-pages would add enormously to our knowledge of music-publishing history, and his collection would include some very charming specimens of engraving and lithography.

Towards the end of the nineteenth century H. B. Wheatley edited for Elliot Stock a series called *The Book-lover's Library*. These are small volumes handy for the pocket; they can be picked up secondhand for a dollar or less, and I should like to recommend them very strongly to your notice. Wheatley, the editor, was a great antiquarian and has assured himself of immortality by editing Pepys's *Diary* and printing every word of it that is not a positive offense to taste.

In this *Booklover's Library* he himself wrote a volume called *The Dedication of Books*, and I have often wondered why no one has formed a collection of books solely for their dedications.

They are not much used in modern books. They do occur in shortened form: there is a notable one in Bentley's *Trent's Last Case*, which is also a prize for the collector of detective fiction.

Generally speaking, however, the practice has fallen out of use, and although this is a pity, the original occasion for it has passed and its survival is something of an anachronism. Originally dedications paid homage to the author's patron. The author's dependence on patronage gradually faded out as book-publishing became a highly organized business, and as the publisher came more and more to accept the full financial risk of his publications. If you are interested in this side of the subject let me recommend you to read two absorbing books by A. S. Collins: *Authorship in the Days of Johnson* and *The Profession of Letters.* The last remaining vestige of patronage in the arts in England is possibly the civil list, from which grants of pensions are sometimes made to distinguished exponents of the arts who fall on hard times.

The third Earl of Burlington, who died in 1753, was one of the last great art patrons in England. Gay, Pope, and Handel were among his protégés, and the two poets expressed their gratitude by dedicating books to him. Crabbe, the early nineteenth-century poet, vainly sought for patronage in a period when the practice had died out because authors were expected to make a living by their pens. Dedication was now becoming rather a means of acknowledging a friendship than of flattering a patron.

You would have to be selective in your choice of dedications, but you might make a modest, and very attractive, collection of different kinds of dedication. The very first book printed in English, Caxton's translation of the *History of Troy*, is dedicated to his patron, Margaret, Duchess of Burgundy, and one of the few surviving copies of this very rare and valuable book has a copper-engraving showing Caxton presenting his book to her. The dedication to Shakespeare's *Sonnets* is one of the most famous in all literature. It begins "To the onlie begetter of these insuing Sonnets Mr. W. H . . . ." and you may know of the controversy aroused by attempts to identify the owner of those initials. Of the first edition of this great book only twelve copies are known to exist, and not all of them are perfect. Milton's *Lycidas* is, in a sense, simply one long dedication – a first edition of it would cost several hundred dollars. In case you have ambitions that way, it may interest you to know that the title-page of the first edition gives little clue to its contents. It reads *Justa Edouardo King naufrago ab Amicis moerentibus amoris*, and it was published at Cambridge, England, in 1638. "Lycidas" is the last poem in the book.

Some books, therefore, have considerable other claims to fame and value besides their dedications, and many of them are beyond our means. We are concerned with the more modest examples. We are interested little enough in an author's name or fame, we turn to the dedication page, and if that shows any outstanding feature we add it to the bag, however dull or despairing the rest of the book may be. Especially bad or comic examples would find a place in the collection.

It will include all kinds of subjects. The *Elements of Chemical Philosophy* may bore you to distraction, but you will find it hard to resist the charm of its dedication – from Sir Humphry Davy to his wife. You will note with amusement that Disraeli's pretty dedication of *Vivian Grey* (1826) was adapted with the minimum of alteration, and a complete lack of acknowledgment by the anonymous author of *Journal of a Tour through the Highlands of Scotland* (1830). And you will surely include *Counsel and Advise to all Builders*, by Sir Balthasar Gerbier, 1663, among the high-water marks of your collection, for it has no fewer than forty-one separate dedications.

If you have a taste for satire and invective you will find plenty to amuse you on dedication pages. Although not strictly a dedication, I think I should include Johnson's reply to Lord Chesterfield, which was first published in 1790, when both of them were dead. It arose out of a dedication and the failure to produce an expected dedication. It is a kind of anti-dedication and also a most perfect example of biting irony. But there are others, two of them addressed to Oliver Cromwell. The first of these is by Denzil Holles in 1647 – a scathing indictment addressed "To the unparalleled couple, Mr. Oliver St. John . . . and Oliver Cromwell. . . ." The other is ten years later by Colonel Titus in *Killing noe Murder*, a brilliant piece of invective. Wheatley will suggest others for your consideration.

An amusing bypath of this collection might be the hunting down of the many dedications written by Dr.

Johnson for authors who found themselves less able to command a neatly turned phrase. It seems as though they hardly expected their patrons to read beyond the dedication page, for the style of later pages occasionally contrast very unfavorably with Johnson's flowing periods. If you consult carefully the pages of Courtney and Nichol Smith's *Bibliography of Samuel Johnson* (get the 1925 edition if you can) you will find all of these listed there and the knowledge you have gained may enable you to pick up the books themselves surprisingly cheaply, if you are both spry and patient.

As an example of this kind of thing I may mention a book that was published in 1739 with a Latin title and without an author's name. It appears to deal with a minor archæological discovery in Norfolk and, except to dry-as-dust antiquarians, its superficial appeal is almost nil. So thought a West End bookseller a few years ago when he catalogued the book under the heading "Norfolk" and asked half a guinea for it – probably optimistically, as he thought. A collector recognized the book as a very rare anonymous political satire by Dr. Johnson and was lucky enough and quick enough to secure the book at this price, a fraction of its real value.

Another fascinating subject for a collection would be literary imposture. There are two main periods in English literature of great interest from this point of view, one in the eighteenth and the other in the nineteenth century. The earlier period may conveniently be founded on the publication at Edinburgh in 1760 of *Fragments of Ancient Poetry Collected in the Highlands of Scotland.* These fragments were said to be by Ossian, specimens of ancient Gaelic poetry collected by James Macpherson, who translated and edited them for publication. Other poems of similar origin were published by him in 1762 and 1763. They sold in large numbers and there was a great controversy on their genuineness. Informed opinion, headed by Dr. Johnson, eventually concluded that they were entirely the work of Macpherson himself. The controversy continued for the better part of a hundred years, and the modern view is that, although Macpherson must have found original poems to work on, he doctored them, rewrote them, and so generally dressed them up that, although they are not forgeries in the sense that his contemporaries thought of them, neither are they truly original ancient poetry.

Their influence was widespread and is incalculable. The first stirrings of what is now known as the Romantic Movement were soon to be heard all over Europe, and the young Romantics read Macpherson avidly. The poems were translated into German, some of them by Goethe himself, Schubert set several of them to music, an Italian translation was among the favorite reading of Napoleon, and Coleridge and Byron imitated them. For all that you may, by careful searching, find first editions of them quite reasonably priced. Only the other day I saw a first edition of *Temora*, the 1763 volume, marked half a crown in a bookshop.

Thomas Chatterton was not yet nine years old when the *Fragments* was published. He was a precocious child and before another year had passed became a subscriber to a circulating library. He read Macpherson and, despairing of fame and fortune as a poet in his own right, invented an English counterpart of Macpherson's Ossian, in the person of Thomas Rowley, a fifteenth-century monkish poet.

Chatterton soon began to produce the most remarkable archaic-seeming poetry which he attributed to Rowley. The whole incredible story can be read in Meyerstein's wonderfully documented life of the poet, and there is no need to enlarge on it here. Chatterton's first editions will cost you more than Macpherson's, but at least one friend of mine has made a very inclusive collection at comparatively small expense.

It almost seems as if imposture were in the air in the eighteenth century. It was not so. The fact was that there was a sudden and romantic upsurge of interest in the Middle Ages, such as seems to occur from time to time. William Morris professedly based his arts and crafts movement in the nineteenth century on a similar enthusiasm, and there is quite a school of rural enthusiasts among modern writers who constantly remind us how greatly life has degenerated since mediæval times.

Horace Walpole started the Gothic novel on its long trail with a book called *The Castle of Otranto*, which he pretended was a translation from the Italian. Bishop Percy's *Reliques*, published in 1765, which had so much influence on Chatterton, while not exactly on the same level as Macpherson, nevertheless includes some "modern antiques" and, despite its enormous influence and undoubted value, it is not entirely above suspicion from the standpoint of the modern scholar.

There was forgery of a different and less venial kind going on at the time. I do not refer to poor Dr. Dodd, Johnson's friend, who was executed for forgery not of a literary kind. His works are blameless and very dull except for the few rays of brightness that flash through them where

Dr. Johnson's pen illuminates them. I am thinking rather of William Ireland, the Shakespeare forger, and of the sheer, barefaced imposture of Thomas Kirgate, Horace Walpole's printer.

Ireland was the son of a distinguished engraver, Samuel Ireland, whose passion and reverence for Shakespeare were quite remarkable. He was rather contemptuous of his son's abilities, unjustly so it would seem, and constantly advised him that the way to parental favor was the discovery of some new facts about Shakespeare.

The boy responded first with what he described as an original mortgage deed to which Shakespeare and Burbage were parties, bearing both their signatures, then with letters and fragments of verse in Shakespeare's handwriting and, by swift and easy stages, encouraged by the readiness with which his impostures were accepted, a transcript of *King Lear* and some extracts from *Hamlet*. His final impertinence was to fabricate an entirely unknown play which he foisted on the great dramatist.

Modern scholarship would not have been deceived for a moment, but Boswell, for instance, paid fatuous homage to these "sacred" relics, kneeling to kiss them with religious solemnity, and Sheridan actually produced *Vortigern*, the psuedo-Shakespearean play, at Drury Lane, where it was hissed and laughed off the stage.

Meanwhile Ireland Senior had arranged an exhibition of the relics, and a handsome folio was produced with a full account and facsimiles of the documents. Another violent controversy arose, just as with Macpherson and Chatterton, but Malone, the great Shakespearean scholar, effectively pricked the bubble, and Ireland Junior was driven to confess his imposture. You may have read a not very accurate or well-informed account of all this in *The Fourth Forger* by the late John Mair.

Kirgate, as I have said, was Horace Walpole's printer at Strawberry Hill, and only quite recently A. T. Hazen has shown, in his fine book on this press, published by Yale University, that when certain of the publications became rare and valuable, Kirgate quietly set to work to provide a new supply by reprinting them with the original types but, alas, not always with the original paper at his disposal. Some of the publications of this press were also forged again in the nineteenth century.

The story of other nineteenth-century forgeries may be read in its entirety in a book with the innocuous title of *An Enquiry into the Nature of Certain Nineteenth Century Pamphlets.* This book costs about five dollars, and if you have a liking for the literature of book-collecting you will find it as enthralling as a detective story, with the added spice that it is all true, incredible though it may seem when you have read it.

A number of privately printed booklets of poetry and prose had long been considered as major treasures by collectors of the great Victorian writers. Being issued in small numbers, presumably for circulation among the friends of these authors, they were difficult to secure, and high prices were asked for some of them. The chief prize was an edition of Mrs. Browning's *Sonnets from the Portuguese*, printed at Reading in 1847. As much as $1,250 has been paid for this booklet at auction and the lowest auction price recorded is £33. The average price of recorded copies is about five hundred dollars. There are many other similar pamphlets in the period by many authors including Matthew Arnold, Dickens, George Eliot, Rossetti, Stevenson, Swinburne, and Tennyson, but the Browning is the most valuable of them all.

All of them were vouched for by critics and writers of the period, yet many of them were proved to be barefaced forgeries, and not particularly good ones when the light of scholarly criticism was brought to bear on them. The most magisterial and pompous pronouncements about them were made by the late T. J. Wise, a world-famous collector, the catalogue of whose magnificent library extends to eleven large volumes. This library was acquired after his death by the British Museum, and a very fine library it undoubtedly is.

Carter and Pollard, who investigated these pamphlets and showed them to be forgeries, do not explicitly say that Wise was the forger, but the conclusion is unescapable by any intelligent reader of the book. Let me recommend you once more to read the story at length: even if you are not a collector of forgeries you will find it worth while. The forgeries have fallen greatly in value since this exposure, but you will not find them very easy to secure, and the *Sonnets*, for instance, is still worth several pounds. At the time of writing their value is on the upgrade.

There are other impostors worthy of your notice. In the eighteenth century a Frenchman who assumed the portentous-sounding name of George Psalmanazar—his real name is unknown—published entirely imaginary accounts of his travels in the Far East, and in the late nineteenth century another adventurer assumed the name of Louis de Rougemont and contributed a series of fantastic tales to the *Wide World Magazine*, on which very serious doubts were soon cast. Frederick Rolfe, who assumed the title of Baron Corvo, also wrote for that journal an entirely fictitious account of how he was buried alive. Then there was Mary Tofts, who claimed to have given birth to a litter of rabbits; Houdin, the magician, who was exposed by Houdini, and a host of others small and great would not leave you wanting for material for your collection.

In case you think we are running out of subjects, let me assure you that this is far from being so – if you have a hobby why not collect books about it? But you will have to choose carefully here, for some hobbies also have a scientific side to them. I would not recommend you to collect photography, for example, unless you are prepared for a few books that may cost you nearly two hundred dollars apiece. But golf, for instance, is a very good subject for a collector. There is a useful little book by Cecil Hopkinson on collecting golf books, which costs two shillings, and will do very well to start with. But if you take it as your guide to the subject, make an index to it – otherwise you will find it a rather maddening book when seeking a particular reference.

Lawn tennis is hardly a subject for collecting. It is not old enough. The invention of the game in 1873 seems to have overtaxed Major Wingfield's inventive powers, for when it came to christening his excellent new game he nearly killed it straight off by giving it the fearful name of Sphairistike. Fortunately the game survived its baptism. Real tennis, on the other hand, is extremely ancient, and to attempt to collect the literature of the subject would be an exacting and expensive task. It is, in fact, among the oldest of ball games. Shakespeare mentions it in *Henry V*, and there is a court at Hampton Court Palace which is believed to have been built by Henry VIII.

Indoor games are worthy of a collector's attention. Chess and checkers again are too ancient. Some have maintained that Solomon played chess, and checkers was known to the ancient Egyptians. Even the modern game is described in a Spanish book in 1547. But if you did decide to go in for collecting books on checkers you would come up against the dedication-collector, for one of Dr. Johnson's anonymous dedications is to a book of instruction on the game. Whist is possible, beginning with Cotton's *Compleat Gamester* (1647), picking your way through the various editions of Hoyle on the subject, noting that there is a pretty eighteenth-century poem on the game, and possibly adding the derivatives such as *Biritch, or Russian Whist* – the first account of bridge – published in the eighties, which you may see in the British Museum, and coming down at least as far as Ely Culbertson's first book on contract.

Translations of famous foreign books into English is a good subject. If you want to see how far this possibility extends take a look at a marvelous compendium of information by W. J. Harris – *The First Printed Translations into English of the Great Foreign Classics*. It can be picked up for a dollar or so by a persistent searcher and, although Harris's information is not always accurate, his book will give you a very good start. He did not know, for example, that many of the great Russian novels were published in America before they appeared in England.

If you have a taste for history there are wonderful bargains to be had, but you must be prepared for works extending to several volumes. Hume and Smollett, Hallam, Macaulay, Trevelyan, and J. R. Green will be names that occur to you at once. I may say, however, that long and persistent search has never rewarded me with the sight of a first edition of Green's *Short History*, though you may be luckier. But there is plenty of material for a collector in this field. Alfred the Great, for instance, was a historian, and you may be surprised to learn that his work was first printed as late as 1773, another by-product of that wave of mediævalism that produced the impostures of Macpherson and Chatterton. The real first edition is a rare book, for it was printed by an eighteenth-century scholar for circulation among his friends, but it does not cost very much when you find it. If the notion of collecting history attracts you read the second chapter in volume fourteen of *The Cambridge History of English Literature*, and, if you still like it, read the chapters on historians in earlier volumes of this wonderful collection. There are one or two snags. The first edition of Gibbon is not a cheap book, but you might easily side-step this by confining your attention to English history to begin with.

Clarendon was the first great historian in the modern vein. The first edition of his *History of the Rebellion*, published in three large volumes between 1702 and 1704, is a most important book. It is also rather rare, but it is not very expensive. Perhaps this is because of its size; large books are not very popular with collectors unless they are picture books. But it is a very good example of the kind of book you and I are looking for – a book that is well written, has played a distinct part in the development of literature, and yet has been almost overlooked by collectors. You see, historians know about its importance, serious students of English history consult it, but they prefer the latest edition with the most informative notes. Thus it is that the first edition is a comparatively cheap book and

INTERIOR OF A SIXTEENTH-CENTURY PRINTER'S WORKSHOP.

Courtesy of the Landauer Collection, New York Public Library.

Ioan. Stradanus inuen. Ioan. Galle excud.

4. IMPRESSIO LIBRORVM.

Poteſt vt vna vox capi aure plurima: Linunt ita vna ſcripta mille paginas.

CONTEMPORARY PORTRAIT OF WILLIAM CASLON, the gr
type-designer, holding his first type specimen sheet.

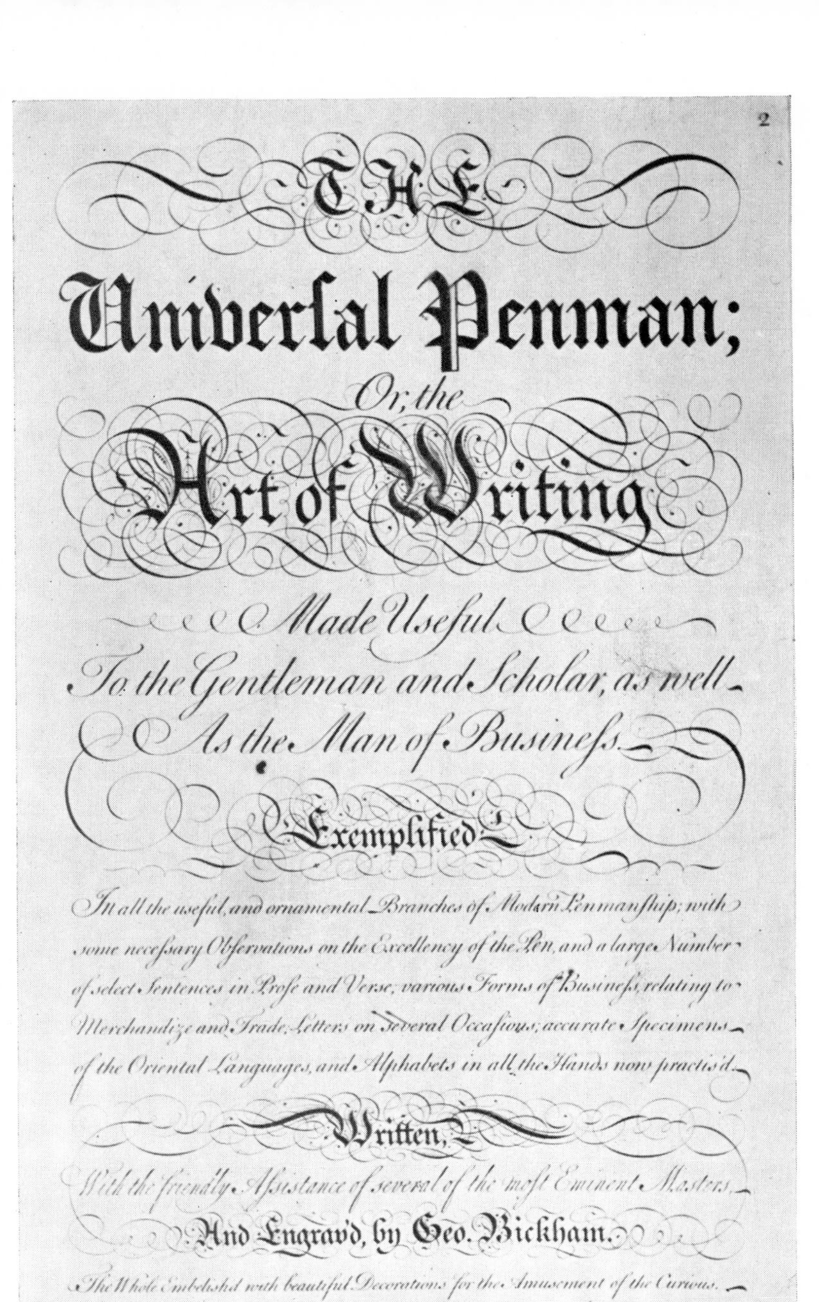

2

THE

Universal Penman;

Or, the

Art of Writing

Made Useful

To the Gentleman and Scholar, as well

As the Man of Business.

Exemplified

In all the useful, and ornamental Branches of Modern Penmanship; with some necessary Observations on the Excellency of the Pen, and a large Number of select Sentences in Prose and Verse, various Forms of Business, relating to Merchandize and Trade, Letters on several Occasions; accurate Specimens of the Oriental Languages, and Alphabets in all the Hands now practis'd.

Written,

With the friendly Assistance of several of the most Eminent Masters,

And Engrav'd, by Geo. Bickham.

The Whole Embelish'd with beautiful Decorations for the Amusement of the Curious.

LONDON:

Printed for, and Sold by the Author, at his House in James Street, Bunhill Fields. 1741.

TITLE-PAGE OF THE "WRITING-BOOK TO END ALL WRITING-BOOKS." It was first written by hand and then engraved on copperplate by George Bickham.

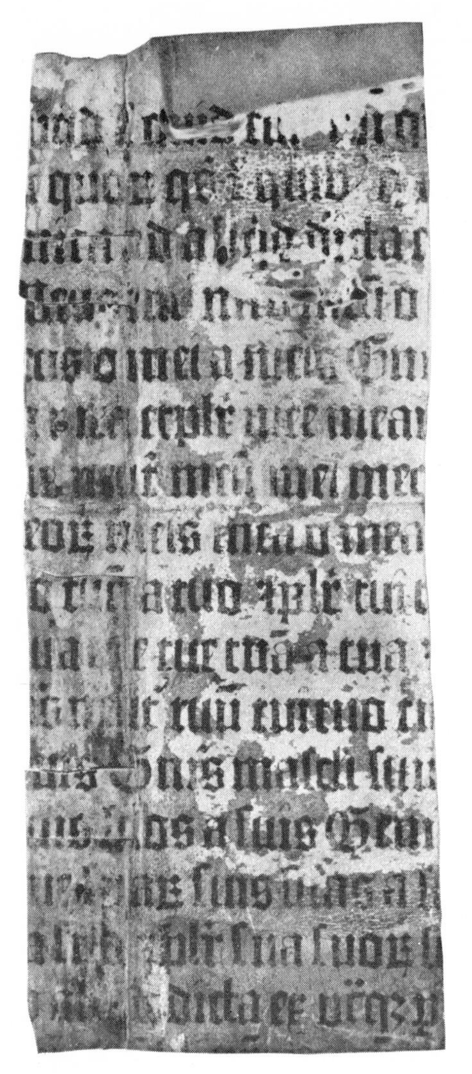

FRAGMENT OF A FRAGMENT. Gutenberg printed the school-boo of which this piece and some leaves in the British Museum are all that remai Courtesy of E. A. Leach.

AINTED VELLUM BINDING by Edwards of Halifax, and the painting
n the fore edge. Courtesy of Peter Murray Hill.

THIS BEAUTIFUL BINDING was executed by Gray and Company Cambridge, England, with the tools shown on the opposite page.

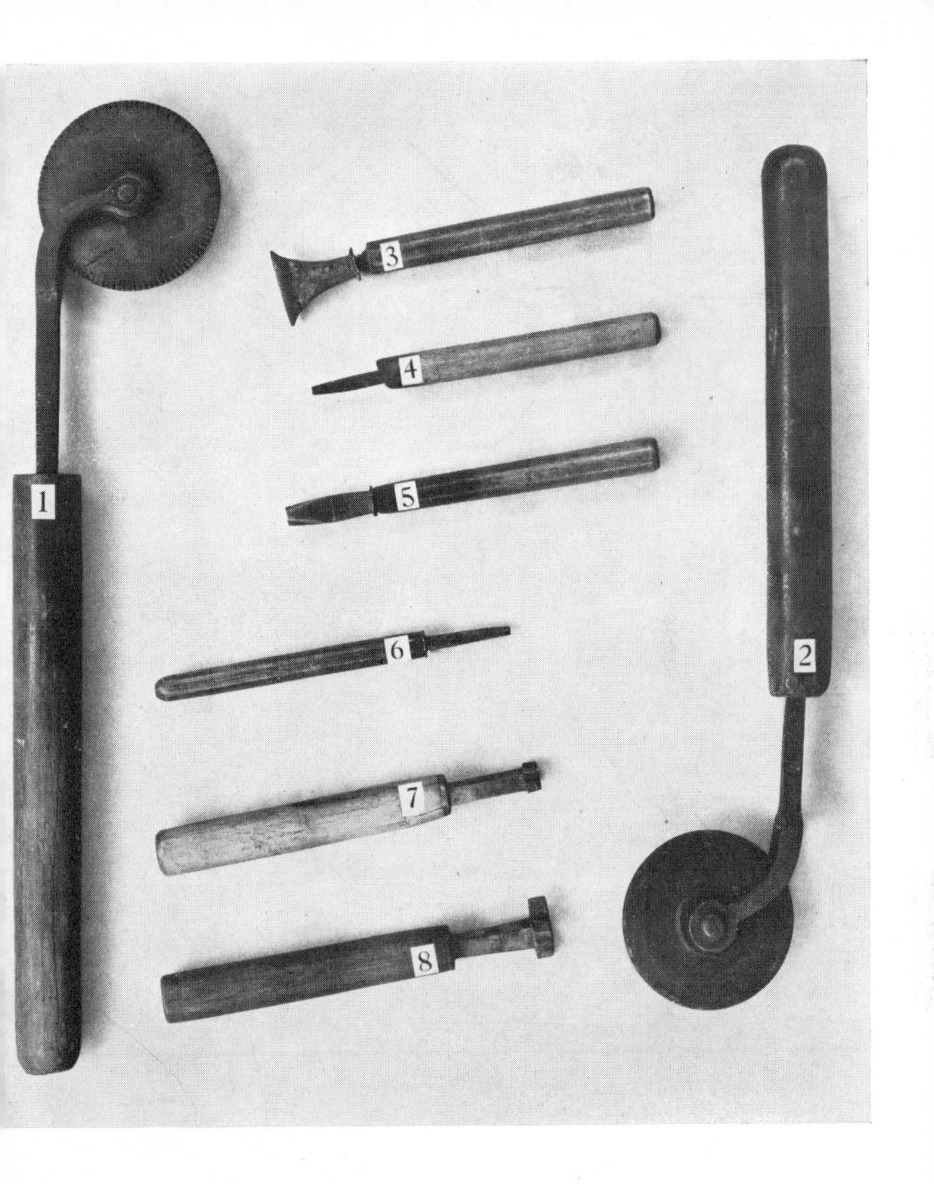

HE TOOLS WERE USED AS FOLLOWS: (1) *scroll fillet, for the decora-*
'e edging; (2) *one-line fillet, for the thin rules;* (3) *one-line hand tool, for the*
icker rules; (4) *and* (6) *corner-scroll hand tools, for the curled ends to the thin*
les; (5) *one-line gouge hand tool, for the segments of circles;* (7) *and* (8) *for*
e crossed keys and corner motifs.

FRONTIS-PIECE AND TITLE-PAGE of Volume I of the first edition of Lockheart's Life of Sir Walter Scott, *Edinburgh and London, 1837.*

MEMOIRS

OF THE LIFE

OF

SIR WALTER SCOTT, BART.

VOLUME THE FIRST.

MDCCCXXXVII.

ROBERT CADELL, EDINBURGH.

JOHN MURRAY AND WHITTAKER AND CO., LONDON.

Courtesy of the Harvard Library Department of Graphic Arts.

PORTRAIT OF ALOYS SENEFELDER from his Instruction Pratique de la Lithographie, *Paris, 1819. From a lithograph. Courtesy of the Harvard Library Department of Graphic Arts.*

330 PLUIE D'ORAGE.

ne se soucient point non plus de recevoir l'averse; ils courent d'un côté, les dames d'un autre; les enfants en font autant, mais cela les amuse; les marchands ambulants tâchent de courir avec leur boutique. Les habitants de la grande ville ont l'air alors de se disputer le prix de la course.

Les portes-cochères ouvertes sont bientôt tellement encombrées que les premiers arrivés sont forcés de reculer et de recevoir la pluie qui tombe dans la cour. Les derniers venus reçoivent encore la pluie de la rue, et tous ces gens-là ont l'agrément d'être dans

PAGE from Paul de Kock's La Grande Ville, *Paris, 1843. Illustration from a wood-engraving. Courtesy of the Harvard Library Department of Graphic Arts.*

"*SPRING*," *a poem by William Blake from* Songs of Innocence, *London, 1793. This page is an example of metal relief etching technique. Courtesy of the Harvard Library Department of Graphic Arts.*

END OF THE PREFACE and beginning of Chapter ("Fragment") I of James Macpherson's Fragments of Ancient Poetry Collected in the Highlands of Scotland, *attributed to Ossian, Edinburgh, 1760.*

Courtesy of the Harvard Library Department of Graphic Arts.

invaſion, aſſembles his forces. Councils are held; and battles fought. But after ſeveral unſucceſsful engagements, the Iriſh are forced to ſubmit. At length, Fingal King of Scotland, called in this poem, "The Deſert of the hills," arrives with his ſhips to aſſiſt Cuchulaid. He expels the Danes from the country; and returns home victorious. This poem is held to be of greater antiquity than any of the reſt that are preſerved: And the author ſpeaks of himſelf as preſent in the expedition of Fingal. The three laſt poems in the collection are fragments which the tranſlator obtained of this epic poem; and though very imperfect, they were judged not unworthy of being inſerted. If the whole were recovered, it might ſerve to throw conſiderable light upon the Scottiſh and Iriſh antiquities.

FRAGMENT

I.

SHILRIC, VINVELA.

VINVELA.

MY love is a ſon of the hill. He purſues the flying deer. His grey dogs are panting around him; his bow-ſtring ſounds in the wind. Whether by the fount of the rock, or by the ſtream of the mountain thou lieſt; when the ruſhes are nodding with the wind, and the miſt is flying over thee, let me approach my love unperceived, and ſee him from the rock. Lovely I ſaw thee firſt by the aged oak; thou wert returning tall from the chace; the faireſt among thy friends.

ILLUSTRATION from Combe's The Tour of Dr. Syntax through London, *London, 1820. This is an example of the aquatint engraving technique, with hand coloring in the original.*

Courtesy of the Harvard Library Department of Graphic Arts.

utilissimam: & inter ortus occasusq; mediam: aquarum copia: nemorum salubritate:
montium articulis: ferorum animalium innocentia: soli fertilitate: pabuli ubertate.
Quicquid est quo carere uita non debeat: nusq̃ est præstantius: fruges: uinum: olea:
uellera: lina: uestes: iuuenci. Ne equos quidem in tricariis præferri ullis uernaculis
animaduerto. Metallis auri: argenti: æris: ferri quandiu libuit exercere: nullis cessit.
Et iis nunc in se grauida pro omni dote uarios succos: & frugum pomorumq; sapores
fūdit. Ab ea exceptis indiæ fabulosis proxīe qdē duxerī hispaniā quæcūq; ābitˀ mari.

CAII PLYNII SECVNDI NATVRALIS HISTORIAE LIBRI TRI-
CESIMISEPTIMI ET VLTIMI FINIS IMPRESSI VENETIIS
PER NICOLAVM IENSON GALLICVM .M.CCCC.LXXII.
NICOLAO TRONO INCLYTO VENETIARVM DVCE.

¶ Iohannis andreæ episcopi aleriensis ad pontificem
summum Paulum secundum uenetum epistola.

PRoperatio omnis iure reprehēdi solet pater beatissīe Paule secunde uenete
pōtifex maxīe: iis in operibus: quæ uix satis maturari queunt. quod ipse cū
multis aliis in rebus sim expertus: in plyniana tamen recognitione potissi-
mum: quæ eiusmodi quidem est: ut semper incipi posse: nunq̃ digne absolui ac pro
auctoris merito uideatur. Sed quid facerem? tot undiq; flagitantibus in nonū annū
premi non potuit emendatio: ne futura quidem exacta post nonagesimū. Versandi
erant etiam atq; etiam scriptores omnes latini græciq;. Consulendiq; non tantum
sapientiæ principes: uerum officinarū quoq; omnium opifices. Ac penita abstrusaq; in
artificiis omnibus: & perscrutanda diligentissime: & eruenda planissime. Iuuit sane
ac munifice iuuit conatus meos: quod minime dissimulandū arbitror: uir summæ eru-
ditionis & sapientiæ Theodorus meus gaza: atq; ita quidem ut absq; illo neq; ego
nec (pene dixerim) mundus hoc munus fuerit impleturus. Codicum nostrorū lectio
ubi in manus hominum uenerint: periculum de sese præbebit nostræ diligentiæ. Cō-
ferentur cum iis uoluminibus quæ prius habebātur omnia: & ex librorum collatione
iudicii censura cōstabit. Quæ mihi sint uisa plus habere difficultatis: emolumenti
uero rectissime etiam inuenta minus: ea sunt locorum quorundam nomina: & di-
mensionum numeri in situ terrarum positi. Potuissent tamen longissimo tempore
ea quoq; partī ex cosmographis: partim ex historicis: partī deniq; ex poetis atq; ora-
toribus īparsi attentata: & expressa nōnunq̃ colligi. Sed diuturnitatis prope immē-
sæ opus illud fuisset. Et legentium plurimi sibi per sese multa ī dies efficient eo stu-
dio meliora. Qua in parte omnes humanitatis sectatores obsecro: ut ad communem
utilitatem ipsi quoq; sollertia eorum inuenta proponant in medium. Nihil enim
unq̃ aut tam exiguum & paruum fuit: aut adeo ingens atq; immensum: quod non
fieret a pluribus melius. Rudimēta sunt: & inchoata quidē rudimēta nostræ recogni-
tiones experiēdo utiq; assidue profecturæ. Quod si in suis quiq; regionibus animad-
uertentes iam minus resistentē lectori Plynium fuerint annisi cognitos sibi situs sol-
lertius emendare: & uetustatis tenebris ex parte īcognitis præsentium nominū lucem
præferre: & more doctissimo tum uiros excellentissimos tum res ampliter gestas: qua

COLOPHON PAGE from Pliny the Younger's Natural History, *Venice, Nicholas Jenson, 1472.*

congregation, over against the table, on the side of the tabernacle southward. Exodus 40
And he lighted the lamps before the Lord; as the Lord commanded Moses. And he put the golden altar in the tent of the congregation before the vail: & he burnt sweet incense thereon; as the Lord commanded Moses. And he set up the hanging at the door of the tabernacle. And he put the altar of burnt offering by the door of the tabernacle of the tent of the congregation, and offered upon it the burnt offering and the meat offering; as the Lord commanded Moses. And he set the laver between the tent of the congregation & the altar, and put water there, to wash withal. And Moses and Aaron and his sons washed their hands and their feet thereat: when they went into the tent of the congregation, & when they came near unto the altar, they washed; as the Lord commanded Moses. And he reared up the court round about the tabernacle and the altar, and set up the hanging of the court gate. So Moses finished the work. ¶ Then a cloud covered the tent of the congregation, and the glory of the Lord filled the tabernacle. And Moses was not able to enter into the tent of the congregation, because the cloud abode thereon, and the glory of the Lord filled the tabernacle. And when the cloud was taken up from over the tabernacle, the children of Israel went onward in all their journeys: but if the cloud were not taken up, then they journeyed not till the day that it was taken up. For the cloud of the Lord was upon the tabernacle by day, and fire was on it by night, in the sight of all the house of Israel, throughout all their journeys.

THE THIRD BOOK OF MOSES CALLED LEVITICUS

AND the Lord called unto Moses, and spake unto him out of the tabernacle of the congregation, saying, Speak unto the children of Israel, and say unto them, If any man of you bring an offering unto the Lord, ye shall bring your offering of the cattle, even of the herd, & of the flock. If his offering be a burnt sacrifice of the herd, let him offer a male without blemish: he shall offer it of his own voluntary will at the door of the tabernacle of the congregation before the Lord. And he shall put his hand upon the head of the burnt offering; and it shall be accepted for him to make atonement for him. And he shall kill the bullock before the Lord: & the priests, Aaron's sons, shall bring the blood, & sprinkle the blood round about upon the altar that is by the door of the tabernacle of the congregation. And he shall flay the burnt offering, and cut it into his pieces. And the sons of Aaron the priest shall put fire upon the altar, & lay the wood in order upon the fire: and the priests, Aaron's sons, shall lay the parts, the head, & the fat, in order upon the wood that is on the fire which is upon the altar: but his inwards and his legs shall he wash in water: and the priest shall burn all on the altar, to be a burnt sacrifice, an offering made by fire, of a sweet savour unto the Lord. And if his offering be of the flocks, namely, of

PAGE FROM THE DOVES PRESS BIBLE, Volume I, Hammersmith, England, 1903. Both pages by courtesy of the Harvard Library Department of Graphic Arts.

AN ENQUIRY
INTO THE NATURE OF CERTAIN
NINETEENTH CENTURY
PAMPHLETS

by

JOHN CARTER

&

GRAHAM POLLARD

With four plates

London

CONSTABLE & CO LTD

New York

CHARLES SCRIBNER'S SONS

1934

TITLE-PAGE of Carter and Pollard's An Enquiry into the Nature of Certain Nineteenth Century Pamphlets, *London and New York, 1934. Courtesy of the Harvard Library Department of Graphic Arts.*

worthy of the attention of a collector. There are many books like that if you know how to look for them, and you may find it useful to enquire about the value of first editions of any book that strikes you as being of obvious importance. You never know, it may have been overlooked by collectors. It is not many years ago that books like Darwin's *Origin of Species* could be bought for a five-dollar bill. The first edition of Frazer's *Golden Bough* is still a very reasonably priced book considering the influence the book has had on modern thought.

Biography is a companion subject well worthy of your attention. The greatest biography in the language is, of course, Boswell's *Johnson*, which is an expensive book, but it is not a rare one. There is always a first edition of Boswell somewhere around in the bookshops, and you can await a legacy, the backing of a fast horse, the winning of a lottery, or, more prosaically and certainly, the accumulation of sufficient savings to add this prize to your collection.

Lockhart's *Life of Scott*, almost the peer of Boswell, will be almost thrown at you by booksellers. Nevertheless there are rarities in this field, and there are also oddities. Gilchrist's *Blake* will set you a problem. If you have decided to collect first editions and first editions only, then you will get Gilchrist fairly cheaply. The second edition of his book is the favored one, because it is so much fuller and better than the first. Personally, I have always had a hankering after the first, all the same.

Roper's biography of Sir Thomas More is the first real biography in English. It was first published in Paris in 1626, ninety years after the death of More and nearly fifty years after the death of Roper himself. The title is *The*

Life, Arraignment and Death of that Mirrour of all true Honour and Vertue, Syr Thomas More. The book is rare and costly, but I would put it very high on the list of priorities for the biography-collector. You should remember, if you are rather cast down by the high prices of one or two important biographies, that there is plenty of opportunity to average. That is to say that most of the books in the collection would be modest in price, and many of the really important ones would cost very little.

I have already contrasted Boswell's *Johnson* with Lockhart's *Scott:* let me now cheer you up again with another encouraging contrast. Roper's *More* is a costly book, but Cavendish's *Wolsey* is at least equally important in the early development of English biography; some authorities would begin with this rather than with Roper, whose work they do not consider to be biography in the modern sense.

Cavendish's *Negotiations of Thomas Wolsey* was published without the author's name in 1641, which is more than a century after the death of the subject, and about eighty years after the death of the author of the work. You may wonder why two such important biographies as More's and Wolsey's remained unpublished for so long. Both the authors had special facilities for acquiring knowledge of their subjects. Roper married More's daughter, and Cavendish was Wolsey's gentleman usher. You may well imagine the avidity with which modern publishers would compete for the right of publishing the authoritative biography of a great statesman recently executed for political reasons. But that is just the point. Earlier in this letter I referred to Star Chamber's iron control of the printing press, and you can easily see that it would not be likely to countenance publication of any book depicting in a favorable light a recent victim of the royal displeasure. These biographies, therefore, circulated only surreptitiously in manuscript form among friends of the author. Even if the author himself were prepared to risk the charge of treason, which would inevitably be fastened on him, no printer would so endanger his neck. Cavendish's book in first edition is not very expensive.

Before you decide about collecting biographies you might read Harold Nicolson's admirable little book *The Development of English Biography*, published by Harcourt, Brace in 1928.

Subjects, in short, are almost unlimited in variety and scope. I could write a much larger book than the present one only on subjects for collectors that have either not been collected at all or have been so under-collected as to leave great scope for future enthusiasts. There is room and to spare for all however modest a purse may be available. But even if you follow none of my suggestions, even if you finally decide not to collect books after all, I hope you will read the books I have suggested to you, for I envy the reader who takes down Carter and Pollard's *Enquiry* or *The Cambridge History* for the first time.

In the next letter we must enter upon technicalities. I will try to keep the going as light as I can, but there are some technical points of such great value to the collector that I hope you will not think I have made them too dry, or that I have entirely drained them of entertainment.

If you can master the few simple technicalities I shall

set before you it will simplify your collecting very greatly, and it will help to spare your pocket, which is a serious consideration for all of us.

YOURS SINCERELY,

P. H. MUIR

LETTER THREE

How to Tell A First Edition

DEAR EVERYMAN:

IT would be quite possible to collect books without having any knowledge of the technical side of book-making at all. Some book-collectors amass quite considerable libraries with only the haziest notion about what a first edition is. I do not envy them, and, if the subject gets a thorough hold of you, you will find that the technical side of it is quite half the fun. In fact, there is a possibility that it might come to assume too great an importance in your mind – a danger I should like to warn you against. There are people who magnify insignificant differences into points of value. They make mountains out of molehills: they fail to see the wood for the trees. Sometimes they do a great deal of harm.

The main point about forming a collection of books,

after all, is the interest of their contents. You collect books because you are a reader and a book-lover. Therefore, however fascinating you may come to find technical differences between copies of the same book, try to keep a sense of proportion. In every phase of book-collecting you will find this sense of proportion an invaluable asset. It will always keep you on the rails and will prevent you from dashing off on wildcat trails and from all kinds of foolishness, to which the book-collector is all too prone.

I may get into trouble in some quarters for saying so, but I feel quite certain that first-edition collecting is based on some other foundation than logic. The first-edition collector deliberately magnifies the importance of one of the many editions through which a book may pass which, to the ordinary reader, seems a little eccentric. It may seem so to you and, if it does, I can see your point.

Nevertheless, I think that the standpoint of the first-edition collector is well founded and presently I will tell you why I share it. But the very fact that a preference for first editions is unusual and calls for explanation and justification sounds a note of warning to be on your guard aginst further eccentricity.

Let us consider, then, why first editions are collected at all. My own opinion is that the answer is largely a matter of sentiment. The first-edition collector wishes to own the book in the form in which it first came into the world: in the form, that is to say, in which the author himself first saw it. If you want a book at all it is because it makes some special and personal appeal to you. The great attraction in book-collecting seems to me to be the link that it establishes between the author and the reader. The books you borrow from libraries, for example, are passing acquaintances. You may nod pleasantly when you see them again, but you do not feel any urgent need to make their closer acquaintance.

If you feel, on the other hand, about a particular book that you cannot bear to be without it, then you will not rest until you have secured a copy for your own shelves where you can see it every day. You remember my advice about reference books. That is just a very concrete example of the difference between a book that has pleasantly passed a few hours for you and one that you would like to have as a permanent companion.

But, you may say, I feel like that about the books I own, but I am not a collector of first editions, and I do not see that I need be one in order to share that feeling. Yes, but if you feel keen enough about a book to want the first edition of it, don't you agree that that is a sign that you have really taken it to your heart? You put it in a glass-fronted bookcase. It is one of the books that you would not lend to your best friend, and if you could secure a copy with the author's inscription in it, a copy that he has actually handled himself, your pride in it would be all the greater. The fact that you go out of your way to acquire a first edition is a special mark of homage to a book.

But don't forget, whatever you do, that it is still a book – that the author intended it to be read. That is where the sense of proportion comes in again. A collector of snuff-boxes need not be a snuff-taker: a collector of wineglasses might be a teetotaler (which heaven forbid!); but a collector of books should read his treasures.

There are other reasons for collecting first editions.

They represent the author's first thoughts on his subject. Later editions frequently have the text revised, and I may say that when I collected an author I collected those revised editions, too, for they are, so to speak, the first editions of the revised passages. But without the first edition how can you check up on the revisions? The first edition is the touchstone.

Again, there is the rarity value to think of. And I would remind you that it is not entirely a selfish motive that operates here. You are not merely concerned with possessing something that the other fellow has not got — although I would be the last to deny that this is a very powerful motive. Surely you are also paying homage to the author and his book by wishing to possess it in a valuable form — by your very willingness to pay more for his text than you need. I think it would be a strange author who would not be flattered by the tribute thus paid him, even though he does not reap a penny's worth of financial gain from it.

This is why some books are put out in expensive and extravagant editions, because publishers know that there are people prepared to pay high prices for their favorite books in a handsome format. I think this has been overdone in recent years, but the point of it is clear.

So far we have talked about the reason for collecting first editions rather than about what they really are, but we have already gained a little knowledge by the way, and we will now proceed to a discussion of the more immediate subject of this letter.

In order to do that we must make a few definitions. An *edition* is any number of copies of a book printed from one setting of type. It may consist of a number of impressions. An *impression* is the number of copies printed at one time. Let me enlarge on this a little.

An author writes a book and the publisher decides in the light of his experience that the immediate demand will absorb one thousand copies of it. He instructs the printer to print that number, but not to distribute the type. Later on, if the demand justifies it, he will call for a second thousand. The first thousand, printed all at one time, make the first impression, the second thousand is the second impression. The next printing may be five hundred, a thousand, five thousand, or any number called for by the publisher. Whatever its size each printing is a new impression, and all the impressions added together make up one edition.

In earlier days it was more difficult to keep type standing than it is now. Type metal was not so plentiful, accommodation was more limited, and, for a variety of reasons, each new printing of a book was often from a new setting of type. In that case we should speak of a series of editions, not of impressions, because each printing was from a different setting of type.

To return to our first example, however, let us suppose that the book continues to sell well for a number of years but that the sales eventually taper off and the publisher decides that he will not keep the type standing any longer. It costs money to keep type standing, the printer charges rent for the space it occupies and for the cost of forgoing the use of the type metal.

If for any reason a demand for the book revives—the author may write a sequel, or events may restore its topicality—it must be set up in type once more and the copies printed from the second setting of type make up a new edition. There may, of course, be several different impressions from this and from any later editions: but any new setting of type makes a new edition.

It is, therefore, not only possible, but it frequently happens that two or more editions of a book are on sale at the same time. There may be more than one edition of it issued by one publisher to cater for different pockets or kinds of buyer.

For instance, Sterne's *Sentimental Journey* is a book that is still read by many different kinds of readers. There are cheap editions of it in such collections as the Modern Library suited for carrying in the pocket, there are ordinary library editions suitable for the bookshelf, and there are expensive illustrated editions for the collector and connoisseur.

Now the first edition of a book is, of course, the earliest to be circulated and is taken to mean the first impression of that edition. Later editions are second, third, and so on in numerical order. One more point on edition and we shall have done with it for the moment.

The author may take the opportunity whenever a new setting of type is called for to revise the text of the book. That is a new *kind* of edition and is called a "revised edition." If it took place before the second setting of type then the second edition is also the "first revised edition." But please get it quite clear in your mind that, without any author's revision, even if the text is word for word the same, and is set up in identically the same style as the earlier editions, a new edition comes into existence whenever a book is printed from a new setting of type. If it is merely reprinted from standing type that is a new impression.

So much for changes between one edition and another, and between different impressions of the same edition. There may also be differences between parts of an edition which are not different impressions but (*a*) *issues* or (*b*) *states* of an edition. These occur comparatively rarely in modern books, but are fairly common in books of an earlier date. I will try to show you how these arise and how to detect them in books you may come across.

The author of *Alice's Adventures in Wonderland* calls himself Lewis Carroll on its title-page, but you probably know that his real name was Dodgson and that he originally told the germ of the story to three little girls. When he enlarged it for publication he had it printed at his own expense because he was too modest to expect a publisher to take it at his own risk. He was also very fastidious and for some reason that is still not quite clear, although much energy has been devoted to attempts to elucidate it, he disapproved of the first printing and decided not to use it for publication, but to have it printed all over again by a new printer. Some copies of the first printing, however, had already been bound and sold and, although Dodgson tried, he could not recover all of them. The second printing, of course, was a new edition and is one of the exceptions to that general rule I gave, that a book is a first edition if it bears no internal evidence to the contrary. The second edition – which is dated 1866 while the first is dated 1865 – has all the appearance of a first edition. It is the earliest that most collectors can hope to possess. Because there are only a few copies in existence dated 1865 – the author managed to recall all but a handful – the 1866 copies are also valuable. Being a book largely read by children it is difficult to find in good condition, and even thumbed and damaged copies are not without value.

However, we are wandering from the immediate point. Dodgson was extremely reluctant to make a complete loss on the printing he had abandoned, and when Appleton & Co., the American publishing firm, approached Macmillan, the English publisher, for the right to publish the book in the United States, Dodgson decided to offer them the unsold copies of the 1865 edition. It is still a fairly common practice when the appeal of an English book to American readers is likely to be small for the English publisher to supply an English printing of the book in unbound form. This is called buying "sheets," a practice which obviously saves the great expense of setting the book up and printing it in America, where such costs are apt to be considerably higher than they are in England.

So this was done with *Alice*, and the first American edition consists of the 1865 printing with a new title-page dated 1866 and bearing Appleton's name as the publisher. Now it has already transpired that the 1865 printing constitutes the first edition. These American copies are the second issue of the first edition. They are a part of the first edition because they are printed from the same setting of type, but they were *issued* later than the English copies. English copies, therefore, dated 1865 are the first issue of the first edition, American copies dated 1866 are the second issue of the first edition, and English copies dated 1866 are the second edition.

The scene of one of Somerset Maugham's novels is China and its theme is rather an unpleasant one. After the book was printed and bound when the publication date had already been announced, and copies were ready for dispatch to the book-sellers, it was decided that unnecessary suffering might be caused to certain people if the actual place-names used in the book were retained. The alternative before the publisher was either to reprint and rebind the entire book, scrapping the copies already printed and bound, or to cut out the offending pages and replace them with newly printed pages in which the names had been altered. There was not much to choose between the two possibilities as far as expense was concerned but time was pressing and both author and publisher felt the urgent need to keep faith with the public by observing the stated day for publication. Therefore the expensive and tricky business of replacing single leaves in many parts of the book was undertaken.

But not all copies of the book could be recovered. Some had been sent in advance to reviewers so that their reviews of the book might appear on the day of publication. Some, but not all, of these were retrieved. Therefore, once more, this is an example of two issues of the first edition. The type-setting is substantially the same—many of the reprinted pages were from the same setting of type with only the necessary minor alterations here and there. But there was a definite time-lag between the issue of the early copies and the late ones and that constitutes two issues.

In earlier days this sort of thing happened more frequently, although seldom on the scale of the Somerset Maugham book. In a more leisurely age, when editions were so much smaller and the entire business of printing was on a so much smaller basis, to snip out an unwanted leaf and replace it with another was neither very troublesome nor very expensive. *Cancels*, as the substituted pages are called, are frequently found in books published before about 1850. Sir Walter Scott for example was very particular in this respect and his books abound in cancels. One can understand his objection to the title-page of his second book, which was a translation of Goethe's *Götz von Berlichingen*, for it gave his name as William Scott; but it would be an ultracompliant publisher today who would cancel and reprint two whole leaves to change the spelling of "reconditus" to "reconditis" or of "barell" to "barrel," which occurred in the second edition of *The Lay of the Last Minstrel;* or to insert a single comma as in *Harold the Dauntless.*

If you come across a book of that period in which one leaf is slit with shears from the bottom margin upwards, do not discard it as a defaced copy, unworthy of your notice: it is probably a copy in which the leaf has been slit for cancellation, but which has escaped the notice of the workman entrusted with the canceling. Hold onto it, for it may possibly be the only copy in which the original printing of that leaf is to be found. You may find elsewhere in the book, usually at the end, the revised form of the leaf and, by comparing the two, you will see the reason for the cancellation. You may have to look rather closely, for the alteration may be quite small: it may even be no more than a change in punctuation. With hand-presses and composition it was an inexpensive and easy matter to make changes in the text even while the book was actually being printed. To stop such a press and make the necessary changes was nothing much in those days and the time lost was slight compared with the incomparably greater business of manipulating modern fast presses which are exceedingly complicated machines.

Now observe a very important difference in this kind of change. When a change is made by cutting out a leaf with one form of the text and substituting another there are clearly two variants of the book, one with the original leaf and one with the cancel. Moreover, faced with two copies of the book, one of each kind, it is possible to say with certainty which is the earlier. Then we talk of two issues of the book because one variant was issued earlier than the other. These changes were made after the book was completed and each variant is always either one or the other.

But when the presses are stopped while the book is actually being printed there can be no guarantee that any particular copy sold on the day of publication will be either of one variant or the other. This is especially so when several changes have been made in different parts of the book. Imagine a common example of what frequently happened in the eighteenth century. After returning his proofs corrected to the publisher the author notices some mistakes which he had previously overlooked. He goes to his publisher and points them out and the publisher agrees that, if printing is not too far advanced, they shall be altered. Together they go over to the printer's shop and point out that on page 9 Mr. Browne's name is spelled without the final "e," on page 32 there is an error in grammar, and on page 61 London is spelled with a small "l." The printing is stopped, the alterations are made, and printing goes forward once more.

Let us call the alterations (1), (2), and (3), and the earlier and later versions of each (*a*) and (*b*). In my next letter I shall be writing about how a book is manufactured, and it will then be clear to you that any copy sold on the day of publication may have almost any combination of the variations of text. For example, some will have *1a*, *2b*, and *3a*, some *1b*, *2a*, and *3a;* the possibilities are numerous. One possibility, or course, is *1a*, *2a*, and *3a*, and another is *1b*, *2b*, and *3b*, but such combinations are a matter of chance and are likely to occur with no greater frequency than any other. Therefore, although the (*a*) version of the text is admittedly earlier than (*b*), no point of issue is involved and these differences are called different *states.*

The first editions of some of Oliver Goldsmith's books are full of examples of this kind of thing and they are quite impossible to sort out into any definite order. For a particularly bewildering example see the account of *She Stoops to Conquer* on pp. 153–61 of Iolo A. Williams's *Seven Eighteenth-Century Bibliographies.*

Differences of issue may also involve changes in the binding, the title-page, or indeed in any part of the book. It may be that the first edition of the book has not sold well in its original form and at the full price, and the publisher may decide to sell the rest of the copies as a cheap "edition" (a false use of the term, so I put it in quotes). To do this he may cheapen the binding, or he may change the title-page by omitting the date, which would give the book away as an old one, or he may leave out the illustrations which were used originally. Any such change would make a new issue of the book, because the difference in time in which the changes were made is an observable lapse after publication. It occurred after the book had already been put on sale, which is always the criterion to be used in talking of issues of a book.

That is all I need say on issues and editions for the time being. You may think it is more than enough, or you may share that rather rare mentality which revels in such technicalities. If you do, and I hope it may be so, I should like to add that I have considered the subject at greater length in my two volumes of *Points*. The first volume, published by R. R. Smith in 1931, is out of print, but the second, published by Bowker in 1935, may be had for $5.

In my next letter I shall write about the make-up of a book and I shall try to show you the important things to look for to ensure that a book is perfect, not merely in the ordinary sense of the term, but in the rather special sense in which perfection is regarded by collectors.

YOURS SINCERELY,

P. H. MUIR

P.S.—As a postscript to this letter I will sum up briefly the definitions I have used in this letter.

(1) An *edition* comprises all copies of a book printed from one setting of type.

(2) An *impression* forms part of an edition, and consists of all copies of a book printed from one setting of type at one time.

(3) An *issue* is caused by some change in the physical make-up of a book after some copies have already been circulated.

(4) A *state* is caused by a similar kind of change before any copies of the book have been circulated.

(5) A *first edition* means the first printing of a book.

In the technical phraseology of book-collecting, therefore, this implies also the first impression. Book-collectors do not include later impressions as a part of the first edition.

P.P.S.—I should add that there has necessarily been some oversimplification in a book of this character. I hope I have avoided anything actually misleading, but as you advance further you will find that the rules I have given are not universally applicable. Printers and binders are not usually aware of the foibles of bibliophiles, but some of their practices could hardly be more peskily perverse if they had been designed as deliberate traps for the unwary collector.

LETTER FOUR

How to Tell if a Book is Perfect

DEAR EVERYMAN:

HAVE you ever tried to define the word "book"? It is not so easy as you may think. I do not wish to go into the subject at any length just now, but if you fancy yourself at definitions, have a shot at one that will describe a book and that will include nothing that is not a book as you understand it. I have tried my hand at it and have given up the attempt. *The Concise Oxford Dictionary* describes a book as a "Portable written or printed treatise filling a number of sheets fastened together. . . ." That is a good basis to start from and it does not seem to waste many words. But is portability a necessity in a book? "Portable" means convenient for carrying, and I have seen many books that can only be described as portable by unduly stretching the accepted sense of the word.

Moreover, this word portable suggests another qualification in the word "book." *Jane Eyre* is a book. It was originally published in three volumes and the fact that we speak of the first, second, and third *volumes* when we refer to each of them individually and of the *book* when we refer to them collectively shows quite clearly that we reserve the word book for a complete work and that our book may be divided into more than one volume. Now, on the one hand, this means that not all the sheets that make up a book need to be fastened together, but it also surely means that there is no limit to the number of volumes that may go to make up a book.

The great *Encyclopedia* produced in France in the eighteenth century under the editorship of Diderot consisted of twenty-eight enormous folio volumes, with over seventeen thousand pages of text and nearly three thousand plates. Is that portable? You would not want to carry one of its volumes very far, and the strongest man living could not lift them all together.

The definition says a book is a treatise. But is *Jane Eyre* a treatise? Or Diderot's *Encyclopedia*? If the latter is a treatise then so is a scientific periodical, but you would hardly call a single issue of *Nature* a book. But is a bound volume of *Nature* a book? There are innumerable other difficulties, but I will not bother you with them. I have said enough to show you that it is not as easy as it looks to define the word.

All the same, despite the difficulties of definition, we do know perfectly well what is meant by a book and, confronted with any particular example, we should be perfectly prepared to say whether it were a book or not. At this point you might go to your shelves and take down any ordinary book. I may suggest a rather well-worn novel of prewar vintage. I shall feel less compunction about asking you to handle it a little than if you had chosen a book that you rather value. I suggest a novel, and one of the old $2.50 sort, because that kind of book is likely to contain all the physical features to which I shall now call your attention.

As you take the book down from its shelf you will probably place one finger on the top of it, lever it down gently into the palm of your hand, take hold of it with your fingers and thumb, and lift it out of the shelf.

The part that rests in the palm of your hand – the back of the book as it stands on the shelf – is the *spine*. It is well named, for it is the backbone around which the body of the book is built. Your finger, as you levered the book out, passed over the *headband*, which is at the top of the spine, and was laid along the *head* as the upper edges of the book are called. Your fingers and thumb hold the book by its *sides* (front and back) and all that external clothing of the book make up the *cover*. If the cover has any lettering or design on it, that is called the *stamping*, and it may be in colors, gold, silver, or blind. The last word means that the stamping is simply impressed on the cover, but not heightened by the use of pigment.

Now open the book by turning over the front cover. Inside you will see two blank leaves. A *leaf*, whether printed on or blank, consists of two sides, back and front, each of which is a *page*. These leaves at the beginning, and the corresponding pair at the end, are the *end-papers*. They may be merely plain, blank leaves, or they may be ornamental, or printed on. One of each pair is pasted down to the *board* which stiffens the sides of the cover. Near the *hinge* (the point at which the two leaves join) you will see the outline of a strip of linen that comes between the end-paper and the board. These strips of linen or canvas are pasted to the spine. What you see are the ends of these strips, which are called the *mull*. They, like the tapes also seen under the end-paper, help to hold the book together.

Now turn over the free end-paper and you will almost certainly come to a page on which the title of the book is printed and not much else. This is the *half-title*. Next, unless there is a *frontispiece*, usually comes the *title-page*, with, at the bottom, the publisher's name and address. This is the publisher's *imprint*. The back of the title-page usually bears the name and address of the printer—the printer's *imprint*. This may occur elsewhere in the book, such as at the bottom of the last page of text, or in the middle of an otherwise blank page at the end of the book, if there is one to spare.

To avoid confusion between the two pages that go to make up each leaf of the book the front page is called the *recto* of the leaf and the back page the *verso*. Thus, there are two different kinds of pages throughout the book. Pairs of pages that face one another when you open a book are called an *opening*.

After the title-page and before the text may come any or all of the following: preface, list of contents, list of illustrations, dedication. In describing the make-up of a book all these leaves before the first page of the text are called *front-matter*.

The next few paragraphs apply to only a very few modern American books because, in the United States, the practice of using "signatures" has been largely dispensed with in modern times. English printers still use them and so to follow me clearly here your novel should be one printed in Great Britain.

Now will you turn over the first few leaves of the text, keeping your eyes on the lower right-hand margin of each right-hand page, until you come to one with a letter or a figure on it in the right-hand corner—outside the framework that makes up the text itself. The letter will probably be a capital "B." If it is a figure it will probably be a "2." If it is a later letter of the alphabet or a higher figure, turn back until you find the letter "B" or the figure "2." This will probably be on page 17, but it may be elsewhere. Whichever is the case, count sixteen pages further on and you should find a "C" or a "3," and so on consecutively throughout the book. Most British printers use letters for this series, but some use figures. If letters are used in your book, and you check through the alphabet you will find that "J," "V," and "W" are never used in the series. That is because the origin of this serial lettering or numbering is almost as old as printing itself, and in the days when the practice originated, "I" was interchangeable with "J" and "U" with "V," whereas "W" was not considered a legitimate letter at all and was made by juxtaposing two "U's" or "V's"—hence its name—double-U.

This series of letters or figures is called the *signatures* of the book, and the pages that bear these are said to be *signed.* To understand clearly their meaning and purpose you must submit to a short account of the way a book is printed and bound.

Books are not printed one page at a time, but a whole number of pages are printed together. The intervals at which the signatures occur tell you just how many. Thus in the book you have just been examining the signatures occur at intervals of sixteen pages; therefore the book was printed sixteen pages at a time.

As each page is set up in type by the compositor, it is securely tied with cord. The pages, sixteen of this book, are then put on to a flat surface called a stone, and an iron frame, called a chase, and the same size as the sheet of paper, is placed around these pages, which are then securely fastened in the chase; this can then be lifted as one piece and placed on machine for printing. It is called a *form.* The number of pages of type in the form depends on the size that the book is to be. The form will accommodate only four pages of the largest sized book that can be printed. If the book is smaller, eight pages can be printed at once, and, smaller still, the size of the ordinary novel, sixteen pages, and so on. In some modern presses there are exceptions to this method, but to deal with them now would needlessly complicate the problem and all that we require to learn here is the basic principle.

Whatever the number of pages printed together, they are arranged on the large sheet of paper that accomodates them in such a way that, when the printed sheet is folded to the size of the book of which it is to form a part, the pages of text will fall into proper order.

You may easily discover the order in which each sixteen pages of your novel were arranged in the forms by a simple experiment. Take a fairly large sheet of paper and fold it in half. Now turn the paper so that the fold is uppermost and fold it again at right angles to the first fold. Repeat this process exactly, always being careful to fold the left-hand page over to the right-hand one, and you will have folded the sheet into sixteen pages, and I want you to number them consecutively from 1 to 16. This should be done with the last fold in your left hand. When you come to pages 10 and 11 you will find it simplifies matters if you carefully slit about one-third of the right-hand fold which connects these pages together; the same applies to pages 14 and 15. When you have done this, open your sheet out again and, if you have done the job properly, you will find, on one side of the sheet this: –

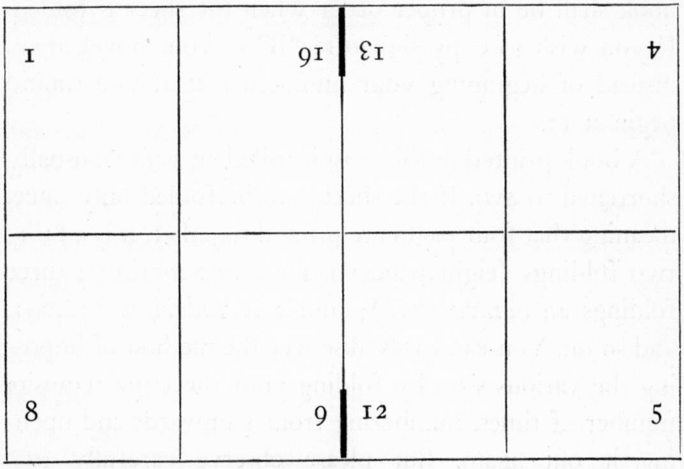

1	16	13	4
8	9	12	5

and on the other side this: –

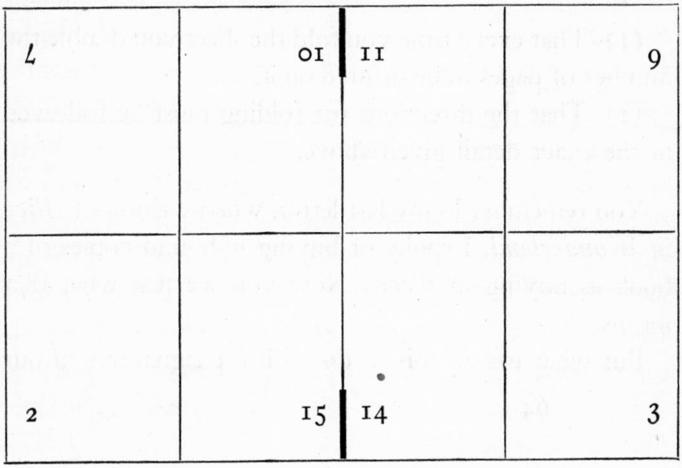

7	10	11	6
2	15	14	3

I have thickened the center line on each diagram where the small slit you made to ease the numbering should come.

These two diagrams represent the arrangement of any sixteen pages of your novel and give a kind of mirror-image of the order in which the pages of type are set up (*imposed* is the technical term) so that the text of the book shall be in proper order when the sheet is folded. If you wish to copy signature "B" in your novel, then, instead of beginning your numbering at 1, you should begin at 17.

A book printed in this way is called an *octavo*, usually shortened to 8vo. If the sheet is to be folded only once, meaning that four pages are printed together, it is a *folio;* two foldings (eight pages) make a *quarto* (4to); three foldings an *octavo* (8vo); four a *sextodecimo* (16mo), and so on. You can easily discover the method of imposing the various sizes by folding your sheet the requisite number of times, numbering from 1 onwards and opening it out again. But please observe carefully two things: —

(1) That every time you fold the sheet you double the number of pages to be printed on it.

(2) That the directions for folding must be followed in the exact detail given above.

You remember in my last letter, when writing of *Alice in Wonderland*, I spoke of buying unbound copies of a book as buying in *sheets*. Now you see just what that means.

But what has all this to do with the signatures in our

novel? You have already seen that the signatures occur at regular intervals throughout the book on every sixteenth page and that each of them comes on the first page of a sheet.

You have seen, also, that when the large sheets, each containing sixteen pages of the novel, come off the presses they have to be folded into proper order and assembled so that the first page of the second sheet follows the last page of the first, the first page of the third, the last page of the second, and so on. The simplest and quickest way of doing this is to gather the folded sheets by glancing at the signature on the outermost page of each and if "C" follows "B," "D" follows "C," and so on, the entire text of the book cannot fail to be gathered in proper order ready for sewing. No need to look back and forth to compare the beginnings and endings of each sheet; if the alphabetical order of signature is correct the order of the text cannot be wrong.

Some books are long enough to call for more than one alphabet of signatures. If a second alphabet is required each signature of it has two letters "Aa," and "Bb," and so on, a third alphabet has three letters, "Aaa," "Bbb," and so on.

I mentioned just now that the gathered signatures (in this form they are called *gatherings*) have to be sewn. If you will take up your folded sheet again and open it at the center of the folds – that is between pages 8 and 9 – you will, of course, have eight pages of the gathering to the left and eight pages to the right of the fold. Return now to your novel, find signature "B" again, count eight pages forward, and between pages 24 and 25 you will see the stitching, and in the center of every gathering you will find stitches which go through to the spine and hold the book together.

If you look at the inner edges of the book at the top and bottom – the part of the leaves that is nearest to the spine – you will soon be able to distinguish, with a little practice, divisions between the gatherings. You may test yourself out on this by carefully inserting a paper-knife where you think such a division comes and opening out the book at that place. If you have judged correctly the right-hand page of the opening should bear a signature. If you have a book that is quite useless to you, one destined for the ash-can, you might go a little further and slit down the spine between the gatherings of the book. By thus carefully taking the book to pieces you will see how it was made up and each of the separate parts should start with a signed page. You will see now why you were asked to be sure that the final fold of your sheet was always to the left, for that is the point through which the sewing is to be done.

In the early days of printing the pages of books were not numbered at all, neither were there any signatures. Numbering of the leaves of a book (which came before page-numbering) was first used in 1470, and signature in 1472; both were first used in Cologne. The reason for the introduction of both is fairly obvious. When books were all written by hand there was little enough chance of confusion in gathering the leaves for binding, and in any case there was only one copy of the text to consider. But when the mass-production methods of the printing press came in, it was more difficult to combine speed with accuracy and these adventitious aids were resorted to. The important thing was to assure that the text would be in proper order for the reader. Some of these very early books have a complete register of the signatures somewhere in the book, usually at the end, for which students bless their makers for the help thus given in checking the book's completeness, which is called *collating* it.

You may sometimes have seen a book in which sixteen pages of the text are repeated and another sixteen pages omitted. This very rarely happens, but when it does it is evidence of carelessness in gathering. The gatherer has not checked the alphabet of signatures to see that it is complete.

You may wonder why the first signature in a modern book is almost invariably "B" or "2." Would it not be more logical to begin at the beginning of the book with "A" and carry on from there? The answer is that this is often very difficult because the front-matter of a book seldom makes a complete signature or sheet. I have before me a book which has the following leaves before the first page of text: 1.) Half-title. 2.) Title. 3.) Contents. 4.) Foreword. Turning to the end of the book I find that the final gathering also consists of only four leaves. This tells me that the first and last eight pages make up one sheet and were printed together. If, therefore, the printer has signed this gathering "A" or "1," it would not merely have been untrue, but a positive hindrance to all concerned.

You should now be in a position to test the completeness of any ordinary book, whether the pages are numbered or not. In older books the numbering of the pages is sometimes very eccentric. It would take too long and lead you into complications to enter here into a discussion of the reasons for and causes of these sometimes very involved errors in numbering, but I may say that one of the principal methods of finding out whether or not the pages are all there, even when the numbering is most chaotic, is to check the gatherings by means of the signatures and the stitching. First of all, you know that the book will normally have an even number of leaves in each gathering because the gatherings are made by folding and refolding a large sheet of paper, which must always result in a multiple of four. Therefore, if you find a gathering with an odd number of leaves you may at once suspect an imperfection.

In this case, you should find the center of the gathering by locating the sewing, and count the number of leaves on each side of it. If your gathering consists of seven leaves, and four of these come after the sewing, that half of the gathering is complete and you have narrowed the search for imperfection to the first three leaves of the gathering. If the missing leaf is part of the text you will spot its place at once, but if the gathering is at the beginning or end of a book, the missing leaf may be nothing more than a blank, or it may be a half-title, an imprint leaf, or a list of printer's errors. I shall have something to say about the importance of these things in my next letter, but for the moment it is enough to say that you can find out what is missing only by either locating a perfect copy, or by consulting a bibliography if there is one of the author concerned.

There are all kinds of special problems with which I hardly think I need worry you here. I shall devote a later letter entirely to sources of help in time of difficulty. The sort of problem I have in mind is one of the rare occasions when a book makes a number of complete gatherings and just one leaf over. Modern printers are very expert at shaping a book up so that this very rarely occurs, but you may come across it in older books. If you do, a mastery of the few simple principles I have given you in this letter should suggest a solution. The rest of the book totals up to an even number of leaves, and if you look carefully at the inner margin of the single leaf you will be able to see whether it is pasted to the adjacent leaf and not sewn in like the rest. If it is a single inserted leaf it could not have been sewn in, because I have already told you that the sewing is done through the center of each fold, and as this is a single leaf on its own it has no fold through which the sewing could have been done.

One other point should be mentioned on this count. If when the printer comes to the end of the type-setting on a book, he finds that the preliminary leaves cannot be fitted into the last form, he might set them up in type twice, and thus fill a form. If he had to do that you will see that every time this form was printed it produced two complete printings of the front-matter. Therefore, when enough copies had been produced to supply the whole impression, the sheet would have to be cut in half before it was folded for sewing. For this reason it is quite common to find books of which the gatherings all have sixteen pages (eight leaves) except the first (or sometimes the last), which has only eight pages (four leaves). It consists of half a sheet. Less commonly some books begin or end with only a quarter sheet—in the case of octavos, four pages (two leaves). You need not suspect imperfections here, only an odd number of leaves in a gathering will prompt that suspicion and call for careful comparison with another copy of the same edition.

All this very long-winded description and detail have been necessary to make you fairly familiar with the groundwork of the subject, but you will be relieved to learn that there is a simple kind of shorthand or algebra of this elaborate check-up of completeness. This check-up is called the *collation* of a book. We will consider a simple example of this in a book published in octavo. The example I have chosen is the first edition of George Egerton's *Keynotes,* a book that gave its name to a famous series published in the 1890's. The collation of this book is: an unsigned half-sheet; A to L in 8's; M is a half-sheet.

Now let us translate that into English. It means that signatures A to L have a full complement of leaves, "in 8's" means that the book is an octavo, and the first and the last gatherings, being half-sheets, will therefore have only four leaves. We can go on one step further. Remember that the alphabet of signatures usually omits the letter "J," and we get A to L as eleven sheets of sixteen pages each, which is 176 pages, and, adding the two half-sheets from the beginning and the end of the book gives us another 16, or 192 pages in all. We know furthermore that the first and last eight pages were set up in one form and printed together and the sheet on which they were printed was divided before folding, gathering, and sewing took place.

Bibliographers, who use these shorthand methods of description, always check their reading of the signatures with the pagination of the book, and the two should agree. Otherwise there must either be some special kind of make-up in the book, which must be traced, or else the bibliographer has made a mistake.

Let us carry this investigation a little further. The bibliographer will give us the pagination of the book and will show how it is split up. This he will do something after this fashion: – pp. [viii] + 184, consisting of half-title [i-ii]; title-page [iii-iv]; dedication [v-vi]; contents [vii-viii]; text [1]-184.

The first thing to notice about this collation (the book is still *Keynotes*) is the use of square brackets enclosing certain figures. This means that the figures within the brackets do not appear in the book described, in other words that those pages are not numbered. It therefore follows that in *Keynotes* none of the front-matter pages are numbered and neither is the first page of text, but that all the pages from 2 to 184 have numbers.

It is quite a common practice for printers to omit page numbers from the front-matter. Sometimes they number some of them, and when they do it is usual to give them a small series of numbers of a different kind from those used in the text. The text is nearly always numbered in Arabic numerals, but the front-matter, when numbered at all, is nearly always in Roman numerals, as though to show that the real book begins only with the text. That is why, in my shorthand collation, although the front-matter in *Keynotes* is not numbered at all, I have supplied them with Roman numerals. There are all kinds of variations of this practice which accord with the whims of various printers, but bibliographical shorthand can nearly always cope with them adequately.

Please note one very important feature of the collation. The end-papers do not usually form a part of either the signatures or the pagination. That is because they do not partake of the folding and gathering arrangements by means of which the rest of the book is put together, but are cut and fastened in a separate operation. Wartime conditions or other economic needs sometimes demand that they should form a part of the sheets of the book. In that case, careful collation on your part should readily show you what has happened and you will proceed accordingly. Such cases are very exceptional, however.

Information on the make-up of a book may also be gleaned from the paper on which it is printed. It is not very likely that you will be called upon to solve such abstruse problems in any early stage of your collecting career, and I may say that, in the course of some twenty years of interesting myself in bibliographical questions, I can remember only very rare ocasions on which I have had to resort to such means. But I think I ought to say a little about this side of the question, not only because it is a definite part of book production, but also because it is interesting for its own sake. To do this I shall need to say a little about the manufacture of paper.

Until 1861 all paper for book-printing was made from rags. The best modern book paper is still made of rags and is still made by hand. The method used is to reduce the rags to a pulp by tearing them into strips and mixing them with water. Shallow trays with bottoms made of interwoven wires are dipped into the vats of pulp and are then slowly lifted out so that all surplus water drains off. The resulting thin wet sheet is then dried on a woolen blanket, size is applied to give it surface, it is put through a press and is then ready for use.

The bottoms of the trays are made of thin wires very

close together which run the length of the trays and these are strengthened by a few thicker wires running across the width. If you hold such a piece of paper up to a strong light and you see three or four widely spaced lines in it crossed by others very much closer, you are looking at the pattern made by the papermaker's tray.

Paper made in this way is called *laid* paper, the wide-apart thicker lines are called *chain-lines* and the others *wire-lines*. There may also be a semitransparent design or a maker's name. This is the *watermark* and is made by incorporating the design or lettering into the pattern of the wire that forms the tray-bottom. The watermark sometimes incorporates a date, which can be very useful to the first-edition collector.

Undated books and music can sometimes be dated from the watermark and books can be shown to be reprints when the watermark date is later than the date on the title-page.

The chain- and wire-lines are sometimes of great value to the expert in very old books. You will see at once that, if the chain-lines run up and down the pages throughout most of the book, but are found running across the page in one or two others, there is something questionable to look into. There are other and more crucial tests where very valuable books are concerned, but I will not trouble you with them here because, if you ever advance to the heights on which such problems occur, you will have gone far beyond the limits of the elementary instruction that is all this book pretends to give. But there is one experiment that may interest you. Take a sheet of laid paper and turn it so that the chain-lines (the ones that are far apart) run from top to bottom. For a folio gathering the sheet should be folded once parallel to these lines. That means, then, that in a folio the chain-lines run up and down each leaf parallel with the front edges of the book.

If the sheet is now folded once more at right angles to the first fold, it will be seen that the chain-lines run across the width of the book in a quarto. In an octavo they are vertical once more, and so on.

If you are in doubt about the *format* of a book, which means whether it is a folio, quarto, octavo, etc. – the position of the chain-lines may help you to decide. If, by this test, it should be a quarto, then signatures should normally consist of four leaves; if a folio, of two, and so on.

We have now discussed practically all the physical features of a book except the edges and/or margins of the text. The top of the book is its *head*, the edge parallel with the spine is the *fore edge*, the lower edges form the *tail.* The edges may be left rough by the binder or they may be smoothed. If the edges are smooth, that is described as having the edges *cut* or *trimmed.* If the edges are left rough with the deckle on, they are said to be *uncut* or *untrimmed.* If they have not been trimmed at all, the book cannot be read without the use of a paper-knife with which to separate the folds which come on some outer edges in each gathering. A book in this condition is said to be *unopened.*

Most people do not know the difference between *uncut* and *unopened* – they make "uncut" do for both. One of the surest ways to betray yourself as a novice is to say "uncut" when what you really mean is "unopened." Always remember that *cutting* is done by the binder's knife before a book is bound. What you do with your paper-knife is to *open* the leaves. So that a book may have been opened with a paper-knife and yet remain uncut.

In my next letter I shall approach a more thrilling subject. It concerns the prices of secondhand and rare books and tries to show how these are arrived at. There is no short cut to a knowledge of values; it is a matter of experience, but there are some useful tips which help to shorten the road and these I shall expound for you benefit.

YOURS SINCERELY,
P. H. MUIR

P.S.—It has just occurred to me that I had better mention one or two things that are not really integral parts of a book. The first of these is the dust-jacket. Now these might be made the subject of a very interesting and attractive collection in their own right, but they should not really be considered part of a book. Originally the dust-jacket was simply a piece of paper or glassine often without lettering, intended to protect the binding against soiling before the book reached the purchaser. It was, therefore, something to be discarded. Embellishment and advertisement were not added for a long time; frequently the jacket merely reproduced in print the stamping on the cloth of the cover. Nowadays some publishers expend more pains on the design of the jacket than on any other feature of a book's presentation, but the jacket is still a thing apart from the book itself.

The other point I wish to mention is the publisher's catalogue, which is sometimes bound in at the end of a book. There is one at the end of *Keynotes*, the book we collated above. I did not mention it in the collation because it is not really a part of the book. These catalogues are nearly always printed on paper different from the rest of the book and are supplied to the binder to be included in all current publications for which they are suitable. I will not go into the subject at any length here. If you are sufficiently interested to follow it up you will find these advertisements and dust-jackets treated at some length in Chapter II of my first book of *Points*.

All that I would like you to note here is to determine, generally speaking, never to pay a higher price for a book because it has something unusual about the dust-jacket or the inserted advertisements.

LETTER FIVE

How to Judge Values

Dear Everyman:

It is probably a mystery to you how it is possible to fix the price of a rare book. The prices of new books are based on the cost of production, and this is affected by the size of the book, the number of illustrations, the quality of paper and binding, and the size of the edition. The last point includes the author's share, and if he is a popular author and his book is likely to sell in large numbers, this will be correspondingly high.

Let us take first the ordinary secondhand book with no particular antiquarian value. These are books which are still available at the new bookshops and the secondhand bookseller must price his wares to compete with new copies. He takes into account the condition of the book, the demand for it and the frequency with which it appears in the secondhand market and prices it accordingly.

That is a simple matter. A secondhand novel may cost anything from a few cents to about two-thirds of its published price according to the conditions mentioned above. One of those conditions is that the book is still available in new bookshops – it is still in print. When that condition no longer applies – when, in other words, the book goes out of print – a new factor enters into the pricing of secondhand copies.

Any standard book that goes out of print will tend to rise steadily in value until and unless it is reprinted. The law of supply and demand comes into operation. The demand from students of the subject is steady, the supply is erratic, depending on the chance of finding secondhand copies, and, as this kind of book is usually bought in the first instance only by students who need the book and are unlikely to part with it, the demand for secondhand copies is likely always to exceed the supply.

Nevertheless, a keen though small public may keep up the demand for secondhand copies and may be prepared to pay considerable premiums to possess them.

All that is comparatively simple: even if you have not already worked the process out for yourself you will see at once how it operates. What you still want to know is how does a bookseller, and incidentally a collector, estimate the intangible something which gives a book antiquarian or first-edition value? How is this apparently artificial value translated into dollars and cents?

The answer is that all the essential features of the process are contained in the transactions I have just been describing. It is a question of supply and demand interpreted in terms of experience. You must be prepared, therefore, for the fact that there is no short cut to this kind of knowledge, any more than there is to any other. In the beginning you must be prepared to trust those who have most experience in such things, namely the booksellers. But I would like to remind you once more that, on the one hand, the bookseller relies on you just as much as you rely on him. Your custom keeps him alive. And, on the other hand, his is an average kind of knowledge spread rather thinly over a very great variety of subjects, whereas you are proposing to specialize in one very definite direction. In proportion as your stock of intensive knowledge increases you will outstrip the bookseller: for, remember also, that if you are wise you will be specializing in a subject to which it has not paid the bookseller to give much attention.

You may, therefore, begin by basing your general plan of operations on the accumulated knowledge of the book trade, while storing up a reserve of specialized and individual knowledge about your own subject. At the same time it may be useful to you to acquire some grasp of how this business of valuation works, how particular demands originate and develop. This may be done by studying in outline the particular instance of an author who is collected at the present time.

John Galsworthy published his first book in 1897. He gradually became not only a popular, but also an esteemed author. These two characteristics may be seen from the fact that he was a favorite serial writer in popular magazines like *Nash's* and also a regular contributor to the early, high-brow days of the *English Review*.

When *A Man of Property* appeared in 1906, both

Edward Garnett and Joseph Conrad saw in it signs of genius. But a further sixteen years were to elapse before Galsworthy's work came under the general notice of collectors. It was in 1922 when three novels and two short stories were gathered into an omnibus volume called *The Forsyte Saga* that he became a really fashionable author with book-collectors.

His early books were soon "discovered," but they had been printed in only small editions, and some of them had never been reprinted at all. Booksellers found themselves being asked for first editions of Galsworthy by an increasing number of collectors. *The Forsyte Saga* took the American public by storm and transatlantic collectors and dealers added their even more urgent quota to the waiting-lists. Naturally prices began to rise, slowly and uncertainly at first, but the pace soon accelerated and it became with the booksellers a matter not of where they could sell the few copies of the early books that turned up, but to which of the clamoring multitude they would extend the privilege of acquiring these treasures. Prices continued to advance and there seemed no limit to what the traffic would bear.

The height of the frenzy coincided with the general boom in book-collecting which occurred between 1927 and 1929. Then, in 1933, in the depths of a great slump, Galsworthy died. The death of an author always produces a crisis in the collecting of his work. The reason mainly is that every new book by a collected author adds to the number of his collectors, and every new collector helps to keep up the demand for his early work. But once the supply of new collectors begins to dwindle it will be clear to you that the older collectors will gradually be supplied with all the first editions they can absorb and prices begin to fall.

That is the story, and, in its main outlines, it shows you that, however demand may be created, if it tends to exceed the supply prices will rise, only to fall again as the demand dwindles. But I hope you have observed another fact in this sketch of an author's collecting history. That is that there are two good times at which to collect the work of such an author; one is before he has been generally discovered, the other is when circumstances cause a decline in his popularity. But never, never collect an author when he is the height of fashion. Planning and sense of proportion, which I have drawn to your notice before, should be your continual guides in all book-collecting matters.

I have chosen to illustrate the process from the work of an author who was still alive when it began, but the details do not greatly differ with any collected author. There is a time when he is neglected, a period of increasing interest amounting sometimes to a boom, and, if slump conditions ensue, a subsequent slackening of interest and a fall in prices. From this point, if there is any real substance in his work, prices will steadily rise again, although the rise may be delayed and sometimes slow.

This, I hope, has given you a clue to the way prices are fixed, and it should give you also a hint or two as to whether the price asked for a book that you want is a fair one, a price that you should be prepared to pay without misgiving. You must be prepared to make mistakes. You must take the practical step of buying or not buying the book and you will base your decision on the importance of the book for your collection, whether you have seen it before and how often you have seen it, how the condition of this copy compares with others you have seen, the state of the book market in relation to the book and its author, and your general opinion of the bookseller who offers you the book.

When you have summed all this up you may still come to a wrong decision. I am not trying to make up your mind for you when I say that not to buy the book if it is a rarity may be a mistake less easily repaired than to pay too much for it. If it really is a rare book a long time may elapse before you see another copy and then the price may have risen beyond your reach. Many a collector has found that what he regrets is not his extravagances, but his economies.

The first point you have to bear in mind, then, is the rarity of the book in question. A book is not necessarily valuable just because it is rare. For example, in scrutinizing book-drives for salvage during the war in England, I saw quite a large number of books that I had never seen before. I am blessed with an excellent memory, especially for book-titles, and I have seen a large number of books in my time. But I am quite sure that some of the books sent in for salvage were new to me. I think it is fair to presume that some of them, at any rate, must have been rare. Nevertheless I sent them to be pulped with a clear conscience, because I am sure that nobody will ever want them. You see—supply and demand again—unless there is a demand for a book, unless somebody wants it, or is likely to want it in the future, it does not acquire any value just by being rare.

It sometimes happens that a bookseller stows away in his basement books that are not on any demand now, but for which he feels that a demand may some day arise. "I have a feeling," he would say if you asked him about such a book, "that that book is going to be wanted." He is often right, and if the day comes when a demand for the book arises, and if it is a rare book, he will be justified in asking a good price for it as a reward for his foresight. But, rare as it is, there would be no purpose in setting a price on it now, because at the moment *nobody wants it.*

Neither does mere age give a book any value. When I discussed, in my second letter, the collecting of book-styles, I said that from 1641 onwards there are many books of little or no intrinsic value. So that it is quite possible for a book to be more than three hundred years old and yet to be almost, if not quite, without value. This again is because value arises only when somebody wants a book. Here is another reason for choosing an out-of-the-way subject to collect. You will be delving into regions yet unexplored, and the previous lack of demand for the books you are seeking means that the bookseller has found them difficult to sell and he will therefore price them cheaply.

Supply and demand, however, is not of universal application in this matter of price fixing. Quite a number of valuable books, for example, are not at all rare. At a time like the present when people have money to spend and not much to spend it on a certain number of them buy expensive books. This kind of buyer is not usually well informed. He goes for the showy kind of book that is fairly easy to understand and the prices of such books rise suddenly until they reach artificial levels. Such books are not rare, nor will they be in our lifetime. If the buyers would take the trouble to study the subject a little the result would be not only a greater stability in prices but it would also benefit them by broadening their interests. Fewer people would then indulge in the preposterous kind of buying that goes on just now, when the prices of certain kinds of books have risen far above their intrinsic value.

Generally speaking, they buy books printed at modern private presses and picture books with colored plates. Anyone well informed on book-collecting history could venture a shrewd guess at the state of the money-market from the current price of a Kelmscott Chaucer. Such books are being bought at anything from twice to five times what they were sold for before the war, and an eventual shrinkage to little above prewar values is almost inevitable. So keep out of that market if you can, or, if such books have a fatal fascination for you, buy them in slump periods rather than in booms.

Values generally tend to artificiality under abnormal conditions, especially where collecting is concerned. They rise unwarrantably in times of prosperity and, conversely, they fall lower than they need when adversity comes.

There is, however, another and very different kind of book the value of which is based on something other than, or additional to, its rarity. In contrast to the books just mentioned, this kind acquires value by being important. I have already given you one instance of this in my second letter. You remember that when writing of biographies I said that the first edition of Boswell's *Johnson* is an expensive book, although it is not difficult to find. That is the kind of book to which I am now referring. It is, as I said, the best biography in our language, and there is a steady demand for it by collectors. It is, moreover, one of the key books in English literature, and it is one of the conventions of bookselling that a key book ought to be expensive. Long before the collecting of Dr. Johnson's first editions was at all general, this was a book for a gentleman to have on his shelves. The reverence for the book is almost mystic in quality, and when you have that kind of atmosphere surrounding a book, mere rarity is a minor consideration in fixing the price.

Boswell is the best example of this sort of thing, but there are many others only a little less striking. What is rather odd is the books that just miss such high ranking: and no satisfactory reason can be given for this. It is more or less unaccountable. I quoted one of them in conjunction with Boswell—Lockhart's *Life of Scott.* I should be inclined to say that the first edition of Lockhart is a rarer book than the first edition of Boswell, yet its price is incomparably lower. The reason for that, of course, is the comparative lack of demand: but if you ask for the reason why Lockhart is so little in demand, I might say that there is not quite the same magic quality about the personality of Scott as there is about Johnson, but, if I were really pressed, I think I should attribute it to the shortsightedness of collectors and I should advise you to profit by it.

Well-read people who are not book-collectors would be astonished at the number of quite important books and authors that are not of interest to collectors. Some of these were collected once, but they have gone out of fashion: others have simply been overlooked. This is obviously not the place in which to list them. In the first place I am an interested party. It would be rather like a man who has found an unspoiled holiday retreat broadcasting its whereabouts for me to betray my own particular lines of country. But there is also the fact that I do want to encourage you to strike out on your own and not to look elsewhere for guidance about the subject matter of your own collection. I am all for helping you to follow it up with all the means in my power once you have chosen. But you should take the initial step yourself.

The second point I have suggested for your consideration in the estimation of values is condition. So far I think I have covered the ground in a way to which few knowledgeable book-collectors would take exception. But on the subject of condition I propose to indulge in a few heresies of my own, which some of my readers may find rather rank. So be warned, to begin with, that some of my ideas on condition are not generally accepted and that you should adopt them only if you find my line of reasoning completely convincing. The grounds of my heresy are sincere, and I think that orthodoxy on this subject has led us into a fantastic position. If you do not agree, so much the worse for me.

I had better begin by making it perfectly clear that I believe a book-collector should buy the best copy of a book that he can afford. Indeed, I would go even further and say that you should be ready to pay more than you can really afford for a book that is important for your collection. But the point I want to drive home is that you should always buy the best copy you can find of any book you want at a price you can afford to pay. A clean, bright copy is always preferable to a dingy one even if it costs a great deal more, as it almost certainly will. Be prepared, if necessary, to pay three or four times as much for the finer copy. You will get infinitely greater pleasure from owning it and a fine copy retains its value much better than a poor one.

Never buy a poor copy of a book, then, unless you either buy it as a makeshift or in despair of finding or being able to afford a fine one, and if you do buy a poor copy, reconcile yourself to its being, financially, a dead loss: you will never see your money back.

Never buy an imperfect book in the hope of being able to perfect it from another copy. The odds against the possibility are too great. I shall explain in a moment when I think you may buy what is called an imperfect copy of a book and I shall tell you the sort of imperfection that I think you might tolerate; but this, if you adopt it, would be a deliberate policy undertaken for a definite reason and it would not affect the general rule that imperfect copies are a bad investment and something to be shunned.

Other things being equal you should prefer a book in its original binding to one that has been rebound. I shall suggest exceptions to this rule, also, but they remain exceptions and they do not affect the fact that most books are more valuable in their original state.

Let me repeat, therefore, with as much emphasis as I can command, that your policy in relation to condition should be to buy the best that you can find and to resist the temptation to fill a gap temporarily with something second-rate.

Many collectors would say that there are no exceptions to these rules and that you will disregard them at your peril. With every possible respect for the motive that prompts such a declaration I believe it to be a counsel of perfection and therefore one that it is impossible to observe without exception.

Let us first consider condition and let us do so in the light of a chapter of book-publishing history. In the latter half of the eighteenth century, William Lane, himself a publisher of fiction on a large scale, also organized circulating libraries. He was anxious to show the reading public how much easier and cheaper it was to borrow books rather than to buy them. Publishers generally did not take kindly to the notion. The reading public was comparatively small and the circulating library meant that, instead of each reader of the book being a potential purchaser of it, several would club together to buy the book and this seemed to mean that the potential circulation would be smaller. The only possible means of counteracting this tendency that occurred to the publishers was to raise prices and, as novels were the books most frequently borrowed, the published prices of these rose higher in proportion to their cost of production than other kinds of books.

A vicious circle was created. The higher the price of the novel, the fewer people bought it and the greater became the tendency to borrow it from a library. This tended to lower the circulation still more and published prices rose again. And so it went on until it became the almost invariable custom to publish all novels in three volumes and to charge a guinea and a half for them. At this price, of course, very few readers bought novels at all—almost everyone borrowed them. Various methods of circumventing this lamentable state of affairs were tried. There was the method of issuing novels in cheap monthly parts. In this form *Pickwick* and *Vanity Fair*, as well as hosts of other popular novels, were first issued. There was also discount bookselling by which the published prices were merely polite fictions, the prices paid by purchasers being considerably lower. But, generally speaking, the system went on until George Moore fell out with Mudie's Library.

Mudie refused to circulate George Moore's three-volume novel *A Modern Lover* because he considered it an immoral book. A ban of this sort, of course, was a serious matter to a writer of fiction and Moore decided to circumvent it by appealing to book-buyers rather than book-borrowers, and to this end he published his next novel *A Mummer's Wife*, and all his subsequent novels, in one volume. Our collector of book-styles should make a note of George Moore's revolution in publishing methods.

That is a simplified skeleton of a very interesting phase of modern publishing. Its relevance for us springs from the fact that at one pound, eleven shillings, and sixpence (the nominal price of a three-volume novel), a novel was a valuable property. People have surprisingly elastic consciences where books are concerned, as you may have discovered if you lend books yourself. Librarians, therefore, did what they could to protect their books by labeling them. At first the labels were modest and inoffensive enough—indeed, they are now collected—but as these proved inadequately protective, the labels became more and more obtrusive, and at last they were stuck on to the outside covers in such a way as to make it virtually impossible to remove them without trace.

We are not concerned with this practice as it reflects on human frailty, but only with the disfigurement it causes to the books. Ex-library copies are, generally speaking, unsuited to the shelves of a book-collector. But you would be very foolish, in my opinion, to reject any and every book simply because it is ex-library. Miss Braddon's *Lady Audley's Secret* in its first edition is as rare as any book in almost any period and so is Ouida's *Under Two Flags*. Therefore, while making it a general rule to avoid ex-library copies, you must be prepared to make exceptions and to accept some books in this condition, and be thankful that they turn up at all.

But I would go further than that and say that you might reasonably include ex-library copies when better copies can be found but when the latter are prohibitive in price. In other words, I would take an ex-library copy rather than none at all. That is one of the heresies I refer to above. I am sure that many book-collectors will regard such advice as anathema. I hope, nevertheless, that you will give it serious consideration. Don't run away with the idea that this means that you should take any old copy of a rare book. Exercise discrimination by all means. Some ex-library copies, for example, are very much better than others, and some labels are considerably less disfiguring than others.

Now what about names written in books? Here, again, I suggest that you make no hard and fast rule. Some names—for example the author's, or that of a distinguished person—may positively add to the value of a book; but what about the unknowns? I can only give you my own opinion, which is that unless a signature is scrawled in an unsuitable place I do not object to names in books, especially if they are dated. I do not like names on title-pages and the habit which some people seem unable to resist of scribbling their names repeatedly wherever a blank leaf occurs is a reprehensible one. But if some former owner has combined pride of possession with proper respect for the book by recording his ownership neatly and unobtrusively I do not think that detracts from the value of the book. Few people object to bookplates and they are merely a more swagger form of ownership record. Dated inscriptions have sometimes been invaluable in settling disputed points of issue.

Then there are publisher's stamps to consider. These are the embossed, perforated, or indelible-inked stamps which publishers use in review copies of books. They may say "Presentation Copy" or "For Review" or something similar, and the original idea in using them seems to have been to hinder reviewers in selling copies of books for which they had not paid. This was a failure and the practice has rather fallen out of use. But over a period of many years it was observed, and the question is, what effect does such a stamp have on the value of a book as a first edition? My own opinion is unhesitatingly that it should enhance the value, precisely from a first-edition standpoint. Review copies are usually among the earliest sent out by the publisher and should a doubt arise on some point of issue, the chances are that the stamped copies will be the earliest.

We now come to the very tricky question of original binding. Here again, before I indulge in heretical speculation, I wish to say that, up to a point, I concur with the generally accepted notion that it is best for the collector to buy books only in their original bindings. But there comes a point at which I would demur, and another point at which I would positively contradict such an opinion.

There is no question in my mind that the rule should apply absolutely to all books published in the twentieth century. Moreover, I would extend the rule to cover, generally speaking, the whole of that period in the nineteenth century when the practice of a standard and uniform binding was the generally accepted policy of publishers. I would make exceptions here where the price of copies in original bindings has become prohibitive to the ordinary man.

Suppose, for example, that you are enthusiastic about the work of Anthony Trollope and that you would like to collect his first editions. Unless you are very rich you must abandon the notion if you stick to the rule about original cloth. If you take the purist attitude and insist on original cloth in pristine condition you must be prepared to abandon the idea anyway, for his first two novels are practically unprocurable in such a state. But would you seriously agree that, because rich collectors have set the pace so fast and hard, you must therefore give up the idea altogether? I see no reason why you should, for copies of most of the books turn up in contemporary bindings at only a small fraction of the cost of those in original cloth. Thus, even the most modest collector may own the Barsetshire Novels in veritable first-edition form, and I think he would be a fool who should turn up his nose at such excellent value. The ace collector may find the idea repulsive, as he undoubtedly would find your collection. So much the worse for him.

In the last paragraph but one I referred to the period when standard binding became the accepted policy of publishers, and this implies that there was an earlier period when it was not so. I hope, in a later letter, to have space for a brief account of publishing history. I do not want to anticipate that here, but only to say that before cloth binding became general, books were issued by publishers in temporary covers intended to keep them clean and intact until they reached the hands of their eventual purchasers. The practice persists in France to this day. There, even expensive limited editions on the finest paper are still issued in paper covers.

The idea was that gentlemen preferred to have their books bound by their own binders in the general style of similar books in their libraries. Books were, therefore, issued either in paper wrappers or in paper-covered boards. Very cheap books and pamphlets were issued without any covering, just stitched together.

When writing on the reasons for collecting first editions I said previously that collectors like to have their books in the state in which the authors first saw them, but I think this is now being carried too far. By all means let those who can afford it and who like it indulge in the luxury of books in original boards and wrappers. My own candid and positive opinion is that eighteenth-century books in the neat calf bindings which were such an attractive feature of the period are infinitely preferable. Moreover, I feel that any collector who has the root of the matter in him will always want to read his books. Now, even if the original-binding enthusiast risked the damage he might cause by reading his treasures, they are much less convenient to read in that form than in good, sound, period bindings. As for their appearance on the shelves, I defy anyone to say that eighteenth-century boards and wrappers look better than calf. Indeed, such is the perishable nature of these original bindings that collectors mostly hide them in boxes specially made to hold them and these cases are made to simulate not boards with printed labels, but bound copies of the books.

My enthusiasm for contemporary binding carries over from the eighteenth well into the nineteenth century. I cannot afford Jane Austen, Wordsworth, Byron, and Lamb in original boards and neither, in all probability, can you. But I would not allow that to deter me from owning their first editions. With Wordsworth and his fellows of the romantic period, my preference would be for the style of binding which is called "romantic." Mostly in stained calf, this kind of binding has characteristic stamping in gilt or blind, which you would soon come to recognize. I would by no means despise a half-binding of calf or morocco, and I have seen some very attractive examples in my time. If I wanted to be really fussy I would select copies with signed bindings—that is, those to which the binder has given his name either in the form of a small printed ticket pasted to one of the end-papers or stamped somewhere on the binding itself. I may add that you would find these very difficult to come by, but nothing like so expensive as original boards.

Before you make up your mind about this particular heresy I suggest that you consult the opinions and the shelves of one or two booksellers. Compare a few prices rather carefully of quite rare books in boards and in contemporary bindings and you will have a little material on which to base your judgment. You may go into more detail if you like. Find out what a particular first edition would cost (*a*) in boards; (*b*) rebound but with edges uncut, and (*c*) in the neatest possible contemporary binding with edges carefully trimmed. You may be surprised to learn how greatly the average taste will prefer (*b*) to (*c*), irrespective of the comparative merits of the bindings.

I now propose to plunge even more deeply into worse heresy still. The importance given to half-titles, leaves of advertisements, leaves containing printer's errors, imprint leaves, blanks, and so forth has, in my opinion, become exaggerated. Let me forestall possible misunderstanding once more by saying that it is better to have your book absolutely complete with all these extras if you can. The only question is, how much better? I do not say that the first edition of *Waverley* in original boards and in perfect condition is not an infinitely desirable possession, but when I reflect that, for the price of this one book I could have a complete set of every one of Scott's novels all in first editions and contemporary bindings, and when I further reflect that, if I were not fussy about half-titles and imprint leaves, I might get thrown in the complete first editions of, say, Jane Austen and Charlotte Brontë, then, I respectfully submit to you, dear Everyman, that it calls for deep and serious consideration whether for the likes of you and me the original-boards and half-titles game is one worth playing.

If you take my advice on these matters you may indulge your fancy in some of the most luxurious and most heavily explored paths of collecting and yet you will not incur the penalties exacted by fashion.

There comes a point, of course, where the most puristic of purists draws the line. There are many books so rare that even the fussiest collector would not blush to own imperfect copies. A collector recently paid nearly four hundred dollars for a small fragment of a leaf of an unimportant work, because it was printed by Gutenberg, the inventor of printing, and because only one other fragment of it is known to survive, which is in the British Museum.

I am not asking you to consider buying books which lack their title-pages, but there are books which are of the utmost value even with this serious defect. Nicholas Udall's *Ralph Roister Doister* is known to exist in only one copy, in Eton College Library, and this solitary copy lacks a title-page. You may rest assured that if that copy came into the market there would be some very spirited bidding for it.

Only two copies of the first edition of *Hamlet* are recorded and neither of them is perfect. One of them, which is in the British Museum, has no title-page, yet already nearly one hundred years ago it changed hands at about five hundred dollars, only a fraction of its value today.

So you see, it is all a question of the point of view and perhaps my heresies may be found not so blatant after all.

I would sum up the contents of this letter so far in two phrases. A judgment of values can be acquired only by experience: but, in the long run, the value of a book to you is just what you feel inclined to pay for it. That inclination, of course, will be influenced and broadened by experience, but the decision will always be yours. You are paying the piper and if you cannot always call the tune you can at least decline to dance.

Some books will appeal to you so strongly that when, after long searching, you at last set eyes on them, you will feel urged to dip much more deeply into your pocket than in cold blood you would have thought possible.

But how can you discover just how deeply to dip and where to stop? I am afraid no one can tell you that. You must find it out for yourself. You may think that rather a dismal prospect. You may think that I might just as well advise you to throw yourself completely on the mercy of the booksellers. And so I do to begin with, and I may add that I do not think it bad advice either. There are a few rascals in the book trade, of course; every trade has them, but they do not keep their customers for very long. You will be unfortunate if you strike one of them at the very start. Most booksellers are average, decent, business men who hope that every new customer will become a regular buyer. It is to their interest to treat you fairly, and if you find one that suits you and looks after you well, stick to him, for he can be very useful to you.

Moreover, although most booksellers have a considerable start on you, although they are at it all day and every day, remember that they are general-purposes men, while you are specializing in one subject. To begin with they will know more about your subject than you do, but you will soon catch up with them, not least in this matter of values.

The position, then, is far from a despairing one. There is every hope for you—and remember that the places where books are bought and sold is the best school a collector can attend. Booksellers' shops and their catalogues can teach you a great deal. I have often thought that one of the most valuable and educative publications for a book-collector would be an annual index of booksellers' catalogues. I am not sure that all booksellers would welcome it, but collectors ought to be prepared to pay quite a high subscription to any enterprising person who would undertake the task.

The more you get familiar with prices, the more of your own and other kinds of books you see, the sooner and the more competently you will develop a sense of values. Some people develop this more acutely than others. They have an uncanny flair for the values of books even of those in which they are not personally interested. If you are one of those people you ought to be a bookseller yourself.

This has been a rather mercenary letter, but none the less important for that. If you feel that I have overemphasized the financial side of book-collecting I shall not plead very guilty. In the first place it is always cropping up and in the final result the foolish squandering of money on the wrong books is always painful to one who has the best interests of collecting at heart. So that I would encourage you to think the matter out as carefully as you can so that you may sow as few collectors' wild oats as possible.

YOURS SINCERELY,

P. H. MUIR

LETTER SIX

How to Transform Mountains into Molehills

DEAR EVERYMAN:

WHEN you go into a bookshop you are usually met by an assistant with the gambit, "Can I help you?" There is a good story of the soldier who replied: "No one can help me, I'm in the Army." Book-collectors sometimes feel almost as completely beyond human aid. Problems sometimes arise that seem insoluble, and, if it is not always quite as bad as that, one often feels the need of discussing books and bibliography, and it is not always easy to find an opportunity.

Book-collectors are mostly sociable people, although there are exceptions, and they speak a common language however widely their interests diverge. Indeed, there is a sympathetic feeling between collectors of every kind. It is the more extraordinary that there is no club for collectors in England.

In America there are several, of which the Grolier Club is probably the best. It corresponds in some respects to the English Bibliographical Society (see below), although there is also a Bibliographical Society in America.

The Grolier Club is at 47 East 60th Street, New York. It has most of the usual club facilities, but its special activities are, of course, devoted to the interests of bibliophiles. Most of the leading book-collectors belong to it and some of its publications are admitted to the highest canon of bibliography. Examples of these are the wonderful bibliography of William Blake by G. L. Keynes, and the invaluable four-volume *Catalogue of Original and Early Editions of the Poetical and Prose Works of English Writers from Langland to Prior*. Some of the descriptions of early books of great importance are available in no other form. It also issued a list of *One Hundred Books Famous in English Literature* beginning with Chaucer's *Canterbury Tales*, 1478, and ending with Whittier's *Snow Bound*, 1866. Some collectors who prefer having their minds made up for them try to get first editions of all the books on this list, but, apart from the undesirable principle that informs such methods of collecting, the task is an impossible one because several of the books listed are virtually unprocurable.

Lectures are given, papers read, and discussions are held on the club's premises and not the least desirable feature of its existence is the opportunity it affords to book-collectors of meeting socially and discussing their common problems and interests.

I hope it shows no disrespect to the club, however, to say that it cannot be considered primarily as useful to the beginner. A certain degree of graduation in bibliography seems essential to reaping the full benefit of the club's activities and its main interests and activities are above the heads of beginners.

There was a book-collectors' club in England before the war, but it was already moribund when the war finished it off. I will not discuss the symptoms of its decline in detail, but one of its principal weaknesses was the rather narrow limit of its interests.

A successful book-collectors' club should be as broadly based as possible and fundamental to its success is the realization that nobody can expect to make a fortune out of it. The unity of general interest that exists between collectors of every kind suggests the possibility of a club for all collectors, whether of books, pictures, stamps, porcelain, or what you will. (Something of this kind also exists in America but it is not likely to be of much use to you at this stage.) Organizational and financial possibilities would thus be very much increased.

But you are less concerned with future prospects than with amenities as they now are. There is a society that is concerned with book-collecting and its problems, and if my letters to you on the technical side of this subject have whetted your appetite for more you could not do better than join this society. But it does not cater for the complete novice. If, for example, you have made your first acquaintance with the subject through these letters of mine you had better spend ten dollars on a few more text-books than on a subscription to the Bibliographical Society. You will see what I mean if you can get hold of a volume of its journal — the *Library*. Take a good look at the contents and that will soon enable you to decide whether you are up to its standard or not. But there are two of the society's activities that are invaluable to anyone who is interested in book-collecting. One is the monthly meetings, and this will bring you into touch with other book-collectors; and the other is the use of the society's excellent library of reference books, which will help you to solve most of the problems you are likely to meet. There are independent Bibliographical Societies in Oxford, Glasgow, and Edinburgh. There is also, as I have said, an independent society in America.

I should say that bookshops are the best school for the elementary pupil. Mind you, they have lessons for more advanced scholars, too, and if you find their kindergarten course to your taste you had better be prepared for spending a good deal of your spare time in them for the rest of your life. Once acquired, the taste for bookshops is never lost. That is one of the most satisfactory things about bookshops, they never grow stale.

Moreover the measure of a good bookseller is the extent to which he is at the service of his customers, more especially in helping to solve their problems. You may perhaps think that a bookseller will not readily bother himself with the problems of a beginner like yourself. Well, on the one hand, a great deal of the information is on the shelves and you can help yourself to it. On the other hand the bookseller is always on the lookout for new customers, and he will welcome your inquiries in return for your business. Like all buying and selling this is a mutually advantageous transaction, but there is a peculiarly personal and friendly basis wherever a collecting element enters into it. I have been concerned in it for the greater part of my adult life and I can tell you that many of my most valuable and lasting friendships have been formed on the foundation of a common interest in books. These letters, as I write them, and before they go to the printer, are being read to one of my best friends, whose acquaintance I originally made when he rang me up as a complete stranger and said: "I understand you are interested in old books. So am I."

Getting back to the booksellers, there are very few of them nowadays who think that their work is ended when they have priced their books and exposed them for sale. Some of the older hands among collectors pretend to deplore this. They sigh for the old days when booksellers knew very little about the insides of their books. But you, at least, should welcome any tips and hints that can be gained from the trade.

I have presumed at the very beginning of this correspondence that you are a book-buyer. This means (*a*) that you probably have your favorite bookshops already, and (*b*) that you are well aware that a bookshop is not a philanthropic institution, but a means of earning a living for the proprietor. You have, therefore, taken the measure of your man already to some extent. If you have followed me so far, you will already have borrowed some reference books, and your first forays as a collector will be made to provide youself with the best of them. If your bookseller has no copies of them for sale, he may have them in his own reference library, and you might take one of them down and show him, from its pages, the sort of thing that is likely to interest you.

Once he has an initial grasp of your interest he may be able to suggest other reference books that it would be worth your while to look into. Let me illustrate what I mean from my own experience. A few years ago I made a collection to illustrate the struggle for freedom of the press which went on under George IV and William IV. I read histories of the period and lives of these monarchs and their ministers. I found that most of the authors of these were simply not interested in my subject. In fact, quite extensive lives of George IV and of Castlereagh, for instance, did not even refer to it.

Then I came across W. H. Wickwar's book *The Struggle for the Freedom of the Press, 1819–1832*, which was exactly what I wanted. I selected from his list of authorities books for further reading, and I kept this book by me for references to books on special aspects of the subject.

I read lives of Carlile, Place, Hone, Paine and Cobbett. I absorbed masses of details about the Peterloo Massacre and the Spa Fields Riots. I became interested in Queen Caroline and the fantastic procedure in the House of Lords when George IV tried to discredit her. I saw how her cause became popular with the masses less because they liked her than because they detested him. In short, I came gradually to piece together a composite picture of the period. But it was like a mosaic rather than a painting. Not only were one or two pieces missing, but what was present was slightly out of perspective—not quite real.

I had already made a growing list of desiderata and I was already experiencing the exasperating elusiveness of some things and the not less exasperating plenitude of others. Then, one day, discussing the subject with a bookseller's assistant, he said that of course I had read Routledge's *Popular Progress in England*. I had not merely not read it, I had simply never heard of it. None of the many books I read on the subject had referred to it. George

Plummer produced his own reference copy and while he went to see if he had one for sale, I looked into it. I very soon saw that was exactly the book I needed. It was authoritative and detailed. It gave, for example, a better account of the very important and interesting figure of Hone than I had found elsewhere; but, above and beyond everything, it focused my picture and set it in a background. Mr. Plummer was able to supply the book and my picture was then completed.

This brings me to my next and most important source of help in solving difficult problems. Remember that you are hardly likely to discover something entirely new. Ideas and subjects from the past that strike you as important or interesting will already have occurred to somebody else. They may not have caught on with collectors: indeed general interest in them may have faded out almost completely. But somewhere, at some time, they must have been of fairly widespread interest. Otherwise they would have made no mark on history and records of them would not have survived at all. In fact, precisely because you are aware of their existence, it follows that someone has discussed and written about them. In other words, there is always a book about them.

Naturally I cannot go into any detail about the sort of reference books you are likely to want. Even if I knew your subject I might not know the best books on it, but you may be assured that the books you need almost certainly exist. If by any chance you should hit on a completely uncharted subject your collecting would have the additional lure that a book is needed on it, and why shouldn't you write it?

All that I can do here is to mention a few books that

every collector is sure to find useful. First, as a work of reference that, if not on his shelves, should be readily available to every book-collector, is the *Encyclopædia Britannica.* Unless your subject is a very modern one I would strongly prefer the eleventh to the fourteenth edition. I am not thinking here of the much higher price of the later edition, but simply of the fact that the scholarship and general integrity of the older edition is on a very much higher level. It was published in 1911 and is therefore useless for references after the date, but there are supplementary volumes of various kinds which will carry you on to about 1922. Moreover this edition is unique in having appeared in handy volume form, and if the minute type is not too much for your eyes, the saving of shelf-space and the ease of handling of this edition are important considerations.

The Dictionary of National Biography is another reference book that I should be lost without, but it is expensive—even in the thin-paper edition it costs over a hundred dollars. But you might get the "Concise" volume, which includes excellent potted versions of all the biographies in the library edition down to 1930 and costs about seven dollars now, or less if you can find a second-hand one. If you are especially interested in American rather than English subjects there is a *Dictionary of American Biography*, too. It costs $15.00.

The cheap re-issue of the *Cambridge History of English Literature* used to cost $2.00 a volume new. It probably costs a little more under wartime conditions and may not be readily available from the publisher. It is worth waiting for, however, and is a miracle of cheapness. Its fourteen volumes (there is a fifteenth, which consists of a copious index) cover the entire field of English literature from its very beginnings before the year A.D. 700 down to the end of the nineteenth century and beyond. Anyone interested in the subject who is not thoroughly familiar with this work, which is at once authoritative and delightfully written, is denying himself hours of enjoyment so long as he does not own the set. You will find it difficult to think of an author who has made any sort of mark in our literature who is not mentioned in it.

Moreover, the editors have interpreted its terms of reference very liberally and economists, travelers, lawyers, scientists, and philosophers are given generous treatment in its pages. Every contributor is a specialist on his subject. You see that I recommend you to put this high on the list of reference books to consult. There is a *Cambridge History of American Literature* in four volumes, which costs $16.00.

I am less enthusiastic about the companion work, *The Cambridge Bibliography of English Literature*, largely because it falls so short of the editorial perfection of the parent work. You will find it extremely useful to consult at your reference library, and you will be thoroughly justified in protesting if it is not to be found there. But unless and until you are a very omnivorous collector you will do better to save the $32.50 it costs for other books of more vital importance to you. Its chief value for you will probably be the lists and dates of original publication of books by obscure authors which are not readily available elsewhere. The American Bibliographical Society is at work on an elaborate check-list of American literature which promises to be excellent.

Your purpose will be better suited by Lowndes's *Bib-*

liographer's Manual—one of the editions published by Bohn is best—supplemented by R. Farquharson Sharp's *Dictionary of English Authors.* Lowndes is well worth what it will cost you (up to twenty dollars possibly), and Sharp's book, which lists the dates and writings of seven hundred British authors, may be found secondhand for a dollar or two. Another useful book of this kind is *Annals of English Literature,* 1475–1925, which lists the principal books published every year since Caxton introduced printing into England.

As I said just now, even if I knew your special subjects, I might not know the right books to suggest, but there is a book that may prove useful for suggestions when you have chosen a subject to collect. This is Theodore Besterman's *World Bibliography of Bibliographies,* a list of reference books on all kinds of subjects. No book of that kind can possibly achieve completeness, but, whatever your subject, you may find that Besterman lists some books on it that you have not heard of.[1]

So far I have been suggesting background books that, with the exception of Besterman's book, are not specifically aimed at book-collectors. I will now turn to books that are definite tools for the book-collector's use. First on the list, because it is a book for beginners, because it is easy to read, because it is cheap and yet completely trustworthy, I would put Aldis's *The Printed Book,* in the edition revised by Carter and Crutchley ($1.50). This has ten chapters and an appendix. The first six chapters deal with the history of book production, the next three with the construction, illustration, and binding of books, and

[1] *The Catalogue of the London Library,* 7 vols., is invaluable for this purpose, but rather expensive.

the last with the care of books. The appendix is a series of valuable illustrations of various historical type faces and there is a very useful list of books for further reading.

I would follow this with Canon Harrison's *A Book About Books* (out of print). The author is librarian at York Minster and combines an extensive knowledge of early books with the rare power of conveying that knowledge with none of the dry-as-dust atmosphere often associated with it. He is not very much interested in books later than the seventeenth century, and his interest chiefly centers in a very much earlier period, but he has excellent chapters on newspapers and one on modern methods of printing and binding.

When you have digested both of these books you will be ready for the real masterpiece on the subject, which is R. B. McKerrow's *An Introduction to Bibliography* (about five dollars). It would be presumptuous for me to praise this book, but I should not hesitate to say that I have learned infinitely more from it than from any other about the foundations of book-collecting. Indeed, while you may·be content to borrow and merely read any number of other introductory studies, if you have the root of the matter in you you may as well buy this book straight away, for , once you are at home in it you will never willingly part with it.

Do not try to swallow it whole. It is eminently readable and can be read straight through like any ordinary book. But thereafter begin again, taking it in small doses. Be sure that you have digested one chapter before you go on to the next, and if, long before you are half-way through, you do not agree with me that it is absolutely indispensable to you, then I have been barking up the wrong tree.

Let me quote a passage or two from his introduction to show you what he sets out to do. He is discussing the aim and purpose of such investigations as I have outlined in simple form in the third and fourth letters of the present correspondence. The evidence to be gained from such studies he writes

> will often help us to settle such questions as that of the order and relative value of different editions of a book; whether certain sections of a book were originally intended to form part of it or were added afterwards; whether a later edition was printed from an earlier one, and from which; whether it was printed from a copy that had been corrected in manuscript, whether such corrections as it contains were made in the proof. . . . It will indeed sometimes enable us to solve questions which to one entirely without bibliographical knowledge would appear quite incapable of solution.

And the method and purpose of his book he expresses thus: —

> The numerous processes through which all books pass are perfectly simple, and very little trouble will suffice for the understanding of them. What is needed is that they shall be grasped so clearly as to be constantly present to the mind of the student as he handles a book, so that he sees this not only from the point of view of the reader interested in it as literature, but also from the points of view of those who composed, printed, folded and bound it; in short, so that he sees it not only as a unit, but as an assemblage of parts. . . . Once he does this he will find that the material book, apart altogether from its literary content, can be a thing of surprising interest.

McKerrow's book goes far beyond the bare limits set by this outline; he takes his readers into all kinds of fascinating by-paths of knowledge in his discussion of every kind of thing that can possibly happen to a book in the course of its physical history; and he does it all with a rarely and hardly attained combination of erudition and simplicity.

You will see how highly I think of this book and as this is an opinion shared by far greater authorities than I am, you may think of it not as a personal recommendation of my own, but as an established fact.

The *Book-Collector's Quarterly* – a complete set has seventeen numbers – will show you not only the sort of books other people collect, but how they set about forming their collections. Incidentally, it includes excellent reviews of books published to help collectors and most if its criticisms are lively and refreshingly frank. It is out of print and rather hard to find.

The *Colophon*, an American quarterly, is too expensive to buy unless you are a rather extravagant collector, but if you are lucky you may find a set in your public library. Its contents are very uneven, but it has many extremely useful and entertaining articles. It is about to be revived, I believe.

Bibliographical Notes and Queries, which was suspended during the war, consists entirely of problems set by collectors with attempts at answering them. The back page of the *Times Literary Supplement* (London) is usually given over to matter of interest to book-collectors.

I rather hesitate to advise you to read A. E. Newton's books on book-collecting, but so long as you take them with a large grain of salt, and remember that he is a careless and inexact writer on a subject in which accuracy is of vital importance, he may not do you much harm. He had the journalistic touch, with its characteristic slipshodness, its delight in stunts and its desire to round off a subject however awkwardly its nature may insist on angularity. For him, indeed, the shortest distance between two points was seldom a straight line. Moreover he was the high priest and oracle of fashion and may tempt you into paths against which I have already warned you.

Sawyer and Darton's *English Books* is not likely to be of much use to you unless it be as a guide to what not to collect. It is the product of scissors and much paste and its commentary is of the kind that calls Dr. Johnson "The Great Cham" and it is a book for the collector with more money than ideas to spare, who follows the beaten track – in short, not for you. But, although its prices are out of date, it will serve to show you what is fashionable in English literature and to warn you which grass has been so well trimmed that it will ill-become you to set foot on it. By inference, also, it should indicate promising openings for the enterprising prospector.

Those are a few indications of the sort of book that may help to tutor the first rather diffident steps of a young book-collector. You should be very careful in your selection of guides for this journey. Delightful though most of it will be, there are snares and gins to trap the unwary and not the least of the snares is the incompetent guide, whose blarney seeks to cover his own ignorance of the course. Always, therefore, satisfy yourself of a guide's true claim to competence. Do not take his statements on trust, but test them for yourself and, thereafter, trust him in direct proportion to his proved reliability. If he is worthy of his salt he will give chapter and verse for what he says, and the very absence of this is, in itself, cause for suspicion.

It is more particularly when you come to specialized

books that caution of this kind is essential. I will, therefore, suggest to you a few books that enter in more detail into individual problems. The *Bibliographia* series published by Constable contains several books of this kind on the competence of which you need have no doubts. They are published by Bowker in America, but several of them are out of print. One of them is on *Cancels*, by R. W. Chapman. It goes into the subject at some length, telling you how to detect them and the kind of alteration you may expect to find in them (see page 53 for a note on cancels). Another volume, by Michael Sadleir, the editor of the series, is *The Evolution of Publishers' Binding Styles*. The title speaks for itself, and there is a companion volume by John Carter on *Binding Variants*, which includes an investigation into the origins of cloth binding that makes good reading for those interested in publishing history. Carter is also the author of a booklet on *Publisher's Cloth, 1820–1900*, which is a good résumé of the subject.

The stringing together of book titles is as boring for the reader as for the writer. All the ones I am listing in this chapter are well known to experts, but, as I have suggested, familiarity does not necessarily breed contempt in this connection.

Forty or fifty years ago there was more general interest in book-collecting than there is now, and the wider public for books on the subject justified the issue of several series of books for the collector. Most of them are still of great value to the beginner of today.

I have already mentioned Wheatley's *Booklover's Library*. Almost any volume in this series is worth reading, but you might keep an eye open especially for the following: —Blades's *The Enemies of Books;* Saunders's *The*

Story of Some Famous Books; Hazlitt's *Gleanings in Old Garden Literature* (but much better and also more expensive are Johnson's *History of English Gardening*, 1829, and Amherst's *History of Gardening in England*, 1895,—the later edition is more expensive and not of greater importance for your purpose—both with bibliographies); Hazlitt's *Old Cookery Books* (A. W. Oxford's *English Cookery Books to 1850* is better on this subject); Wheatley's *How to Form a Library;* Matthew's *The Literature of Music*, and Lawler's *Book Auctions in England.*

Richard Garnett's *Library Series* is more suitable for librarians than for collectors. One of them, however, is well worth your while. This is H. B. Wheatley's *Prices of Books.* The subject is too vast to be covered in a pocket volume and much has been discovered about the published prices of books since Wheatley wrote in 1898. But there is a great deal of amusing and interesting material about the fluctuating values of rare books at different periods.

A. W. Pollard has not only written a great deal about old books himself, but he has edited two series of books for book-collectors. The earlier of the two is the *Books about Books* series. This includes Gordon Duff's *Early Printed Books;* H. P. Horne's *Book-Bindings;* F. Madan's *Books in Manuscript* and C. and M. Elton's *The Great Book Collectors.*

The last of these has been superseded to some extent by W. Y. Fletcher's *English Book Collectors*, in Pollard's other series, the *English Bookman's Library*, but better than either is Seymour de Ricci's *English Collectors of Books and Manuscripts (1530–1930) and their Marks of Ownership* (Cambridge: University Press).

I could go on for a long time in this way, and I could obviously have got in more titles if I had made a list of books instead of writing you a letter about some of them. But I always find such lists rather bewildering myself, because I am never quite sure whether the compiler has gone on the principle of cramming in all he can on the subject, or whether the list is really a recommended one. So I thought you would prefer to have a little detail about just a few books.

I could be very much at home in a collection of books about books. This would be a good subject to collect—but not a cheap one. Some reference books are very expensive. In my recommendations, however, you will not find any of these. I have put the new price of recently published books in brackets after each. Many of them may be out of print, but the published price will be a guide to their likely secondhand cost.

YOURS SINCERELY,

P. H. MUIR

LETTER SEVEN

How to Read a Bookseller's Catalogue

DEAR EVERYMAN:

YOUR English counterpart received my little book with great kindness; its wide circulation and the high praises it has received from critics and the general public have greatly exceeded the hopes of its gratified author. It is even more gratifying to see it in American dress, for some of my best friends among bibliophiles are in America and my experience with them makes me look forward pleasurably to increasing their number in this manner.

I hope that one of the results of your having read the original edition has been that you have added your name to some bookseller's mailing list to receive his catalogues. If you have done this and have received a catalogue, I can imagine that if it is your first you may be wondering how to interpret the abbreviations and technical terms, some of which appear in every bookseller's catalogue. I have decided, therefore, to devote this extra letter to elucidating the terms in more general use by cataloguers so as to help you to picture more clearly the books you find described there.

A bookseller issues catalogues to give some notion of his stock to distant customers who are unable to visit his premises and inspect it for themselves. The catalogue should give the author of the book, where that is known, its title, date, size, binding, condition, and price. If it has features of interest that do not appear on the surface these may be added in a note, more or less elaborate, after all the above information has been supplied.

There are some features of cataloguing that most booksellers regard as indispensable, such as listing books alphabetically under author or subject, with a cross-index from one to the other; and, especially, the consecutive numbering of the items. Booksellers who ignore such things—and some do—appear to want to make things as difficult as possible for their customers, and to defeat the principal object for which the catalogue is issued, which is to sell the books in it. A catalogue in which the items are not numbered is an abomination, as you will soon discover if you try to order from it by telegram.

Alphabetical order makes it easier to select from a catalogue and although chronological order is more suitable for some purposes, this should always be supplemented by a good alphabetical index. But this is advice to booksellers which it is not my business to offer. One piece of advice I would urge upon you is not to skip too readily sections of a catalogue which you think unlikely to interest you. Remember the expert mentioned on p. 30, who secured a notable first edition very cheaply because he did not skip the topographical section of a catalogue.

Let us now analyze the construction of the catalogue in accordance with the brief outline given above. First comes the author's name. This is generally transcribed from the title-page of the book, but many books were originally issued anonymously or under a pseudonym. Political or personal reasons have sometimes made anonymity advisable. In earlier times it was not considered quite nice for a gentlewoman to write books and to take money for doing so. Thus Jane Austen's novels do not bear her name on the title-pages of the original editions; they are described as "By a lady." Charlotte Brontë thought that her novels would reach a wider public if they were taken to be the work of a man, so she called herself "Currer Bell" and her sisters, Anne and Emily, used the same surname with the given names Acton and Ellis. Mary Ann Evans called herself George Eliot.

The usual method of signifying to the reader of a catalogue that a book is anonymous or pseudonymous is to put the author's real name, within square brackets, thus:—[AUSTEN (Jane)]; or [BRONTË (Charlotte)].

There is, by the way, no general rule about the place in the catalogue where the pseudonymous works of an author should be listed, but there are conventions about it which you will readily learn from the study of a few catalogues. Authors who published their books anonymously are, of course, listed under their real names; thus Jane Austen always appears among the "A's." But whereas the Brontës are always catalogued under their real names, George Eliot is almost invariably catalogued under her pseudonym and very few booksellers take the trouble to mention her real name at all. This is to accord with the general method of referring to their favorites which readers and collectors use. For example, no one would dream of saying that he collected "the Bells" when he meant the Brontës, but it is George Eliot who is collected, not Miss Evans. The real name of "Phiz," who acquired fame when he illustrated *Pickwick*, was Hablot K. Browne, but when his real name occurs on a title-page he may still be referred to by the bookseller as [Phiz] to remind you of his more familiar alter ego. Some authors are listed sometimes under their real names and sometimes under their psuedonyms. One of them is "Mark Rutherford," whose real name was W. Hale White. These are tricks of the trade which you will pick up as you go along.

A cataloguer uses these square brackets whenever he wishes to convey that what is contained within them is not printed in the book he is describing but is added from his own knowledge of the facts. The information may refer to the author, title, publisher, place of publication, or date of the book. There are exceptions to this rule in regard to early printed books, but you will not be likely to be bothered with these for some time to come and when you are you should consult a specialist work on the subject.

Next will come the title of the book and here catalogue practice may differ very considerably, especially as to the extent to which early, long-winded titles are transcribed. For instance the original title of what you and I know as *Pickwick Papers* was *The Posthumous Papers of the Pickwick Club, containing a faithful record of the Perambulations, Perils, Travels, Adventures and Sporting Transactions of the Corresponding Members.* What you and I call

Gulliver's Travels was entitled by its author *Travels into Several Remote Nations of the World.* The further in time you go back, generally speaking, the lengthier and more involved the title becomes and you are also confronted by instances where the whim of a translator produces considerable variations in the wording of a title. For instance, when Shelton first translated Cervantes's great novel into English in 1612 he called it *The History of the valorous and witty Knight Errant Don Quixote,* but when he added the second part in 1620 and reprinted the first part to go with it he called it *The History of Don-Quichote.* When Jarvis came to translate the book in 1742 he called it *Life and Exploits of the ingenious Gentleman Don Quixote de la Mancha,* and so it went on. There are books by seventeenth-century writers like John Dunton, the titles of each of which would almost fill one page of an ordinary bookseller's catalogue. Every bookseller will abbreviate such titles in his own way, balancing economy against the desire to describe the book as fully as possible.

We now come to the edition of the book, which should be specified if it is of importance. Above all, of course, first editions should be so described if the fact is significant. Furthermore, if variants of the book are known, the catalogue should say to which of these the copy conforms; usually it will add a note giving the points of issue, and it will be to your interest to check these against your own knowledge of the bibliography of the book. Because here, again, bookselling practice differs very widely on the amount of detail that should be provided about points of issue. Some booksellers although they would emphasize the fact when a book is the first issue would not consider it incumbent upon them to mention the fact if it was a later issue. My own opinion is that if the catalogue does not qualify the expression "first edition" in some way, then the reader is entitled to expect the earliest known issue of the book, but this is certainly not an opinion universally shared by booksellers. Therefore, if you find a book catalogued simply as a first edition and you know that there are variants it will pay you to specify in your order that the book is to be sent only if it is of the variant that you require, otherwise you may suffer a major disappointment and find yourself not entitled to return the book on grounds of misdescription.

It is also my opinion that it is bad form for a cataloguer to indulge in special pleading about later issues in some such words as these: "This is not, of course, the extremely rare first issue of which only *x* copies are known, and which is worth *y* times the price asked for our copy." This sort of thing arouses sales-resistance in me and I do not advise you to be the more inclined to buy a book because of reasoning along those lines.

Next comes the binding, about which there is a great deal to be said, for it is here the cataloguer, try as he will, is inevitably unable to give anything like a complete picture of the book. Whether its condition is the finest it is possible to imagine, or whether it has defects, a catalogue description is inadequate to convey the actual facts of the case. I have often looked at a book that I have gladly bought and thought to myself that if I had seen its faults carefully listed in detail in a catalogue I would never have thought of buying it; the mere listing of its tiny deficiencies and stains would have made it seem appalling, although actually it is quite a good copy. To a great extent, therefore, you must get to know your bookseller and his habits. What one bookseller will describe as a fine copy, another will call only good, and, at the other extreme, I have had books sent me that were described as good copies that turned out, on arrival, to be so disgustingly filthy that I have hardly liked to touch them without tongs. Some booksellers collate their books, others take it for granted that they are perfect. Generally speaking, however, booksellers are no more unreasonable than the ordinary run of mankind, and they will take back books you have ordered if they do not come up to your expectations, so long as you return them quickly. Some booksellers are unreasonable about this and make a fuss if you return a book on any grounds whatsoever. One transaction with such a bookseller will probably be enough for you; it always is for me.

Very often you will find somewhere in a bookseller's catalogue a statement of the terms on which he is prepared to do business from his catalogue. Here is an extract from one of them. "All books in this catalogue are in their original bindings, complete, and in good condition, unless otherwise stated. The return of any book for reasons of misdescription will be accepted if promptly made." That is perfectly clear and tells you the grounds on which you are entitled to return a book. Never overlook, or fail to familiarize yourself with such statements and always, for your own part, observe such conditions rigidly. They are made as much for your protection as for the bookseller himself and as it is his book that you are ordering you must be prepared to abide by the conditions he has made; by the very fact of ordering a book from his catalogue you have implicitly undertaken to deal in accordance with the terms he has set down. I have already indicated that you will do well to avoid a bookseller who tries to be clever with you, but beware, equally, of attempting funny tricks or cheap scores yourself. Always try, in fact, to get on good terms with the booksellers; it will pay you in the end. Apart altogether from the right to return a book because it does not come up to the catalogue description you may also order books on approval and this entitles you to return them without giving any reason at all, although it is more satisfactory to say why you are doing so. Moreover you must return unwanted books within a definite time, usually within four days of receiving them, and you should pay postage both ways. Naturally, if the bookseller has a definite order for the book from another client he will not send it on approval to you; and when a catalogue is first issued he will be reluctant to send books from it on approval for a few days in case definite orders arrive in the meantime.

It is important to acquaint yourself with the bookseller's practice in describing original bindings. The extract I have quoted above tells you quite definitely that you may expect the books to be in original binding unless the catalogue says they are not. Some cataloguers, while omitting this phrase, do, nevertheless accept its implications, while others do not. Thus there are booksellers who when they describe the binding as "cloth" without further qualification mean that the book is rebound. If you are in any doubt on this point you had better specify in your order that you do not want the book unless the binding is original, after this fashion: "Please send . . . if in original binding." This, I repeat, is very important if you are in any doubt.

Another cataloguing convention that concerns original condition is the use of the word "unbound." Many a pamphlet or small book was originally issued with no binding at all, but "unbound" in a secondhand catalogue may mean exactly what it says and no more. A publication that was originally issued without any cover, even a wrapper, and which is now offered in that state would probably be described as "stitched (or sewn) as issued," the last two words forming the operative clause. The book may be stitched, or sewn (i.e. with thread), wired, or stabbed.

Wiring, or wire-stapling was the first method of stitching a book by machinery generally available to binders. It was introduced in the United States in about 1875 but it was very unsatisfactory and was soon ousted by another American invention—a machine that would sew books with thread. Stabbing was much in vogue in the nineteenth century when novels, and occasionally also non-fictional works, were issued in periodical parts. If you examine the inner margins of some of these parts you will see two or three small slits running right through. These are the stab-holes, a cheap method of securing the leaves of each part to answer a temporary purpose. They are something to look for in bound copies, even in original bindings, of books first issued in parts and afterwards in volume form. It was customary to conclude the part issue of a work with a double number which contained, among other things, a title-page, and lists of contents and illustrations to the whole work. Subscribers were then invited to have their parts put up in covers which could be bought from the publisher in cloth or leather in much the same way as is done with modern part issues like *The History of the World* or *People of all Nations*.

Dickens, Thackeray, Trollope, and other writers of the

period had some of their works issued in this way. Part issues attract collectors very strongly and as they are naturally rare when complete and perfect they are sometimes very expensive. They are desirable not only because of their rarity but also because they are usually, although not invariably, the form in which the book was first issued. No other branch of book-collecting offers more opportunity for wrong-headedness by collectors than the craze for part issues and, although this is not the place to discuss it at any length, I think you should be on your guard against being led into extravagances of this kind.

The next earliest thing to a set of the parts themselves is a copy bound from them because this will contain a reasonably early state of the text and the plates. If you would like to know how very greatly these may vary in different states of the same book you should look into the bewildering publishing history of *Pickwick* in Hatton and Cleaver's *Bibliography of the Periodical Works of Charles Dickens*, Chapman and Hall, 1933. The description of this one work occupies nearly ninety pages of a large book, but you should take with a grain or two of salt what the authors have to say about advertisements, inset or otherwise.

The fact that a book has been bound from the parts is most readily observable from the stab-holes in the margins and as the illustrations were usually on different paper from the text, and do not, therefore, form part of the signatures; they were occasionally turned about in the bound copies and may have the stab-holes on the outer margins, which is often the easiest way of verifying their part origin. With *Pickwick*, so great were the alterations made while the book was still running in parts, that it would be a miracle to find a bound copy in the earliest state throughout unless it has been "doctored," and this applies to the majority of part sets also. A better example of the desirability of copies bound from the parts is given by Sadleir in relation to Trollope's *Orley Farm* where he shows that the only way of being quite sure of a first state of the book is to find one with stab-holes on every page.

Returning now to the actual binding, in Letter V there is a reference to the practice before 1800 of issuing books in temporary covers of either paper boards or wrappers and I said that booksellers or publishers also offered them in leather bindings for those who preferred to buy their books already bound. It is possible with some degree of certainty to identify styles of eighteenth-century leather binding as of this kind, and it is quite reasonable to describe such bindings as original. The practice is inadvisable, however, for reasons which cannot be detailed here, but which may be summarized by saying that the conventions of publishing practice were not sufficiently regularized at the time. You will be well advised, therefore, to regard the use of the word "original" in connection with any form of leather binding as interchangeable with "contemporary." Thus you would interpret "original calf" on an eighteenth-century book as meaning that it was bound in calf at about the time of publication, not necessarily by the publisher. Of course, many books have been issued in leather bindings by their publishers, but these are in a different category, which you will come to recognize by experience.

There is one other bibliographical tip in connection with original binding that it is useful to remember. This entails some familiarity with the history of binding styles, and one or two examples of the sort of thing I mean will suffice to suggest how useful it may be in reading catalogues. I have mentioned, on p. 24, that cloth was introduced in about 1825. If, therefore, you see a book dated, say, 1800, described as in "original" or "publisher's" cloth, you may be sure that it is a late issue of the binding (*a*) because when the book was originally published cloth was not yet in use by publishers and (*b*) because this copy could not have been issued before about 1825, which is twenty-five years after the date on the title-page. "Half-cloth" means that the spine and a part of the sides are of cloth, the rest of the sides being of some other material, probably paper-covered boards. This is a style that was very popular in the 1830's, and it persisted for some time after the introduction of full cloth with gilt stamping. Sometimes publishers issued the same book in alternative styles – half- and full-cloth. Sadleir (see p. 113) illustrates the history of this style between about 1832 and 1842. So that half-cloth is unlikely to be the original binding before 1830, but it is quite common thereafter for the next ten years or so.

Another point on original cloth that I should like to mention concerns books taken over by one publisher from another. Conan Doyle's *The Sign of Four* was published originally by Spencer Blackett, whose business was taken over eventually by Griffith and Farran, who reissued the original sheets with Spencer Blackett's name on the title-page but with their own imprint on the binding. Clearly a Griffith and Farran copy of the book, although not a first issue, would not be returnable on the grounds that it was not in original cloth. There are many examples of this kind which call for a special knowledge of the books in question—a knowledge with which you will certainly provide yourself if they come within your collecting ken.

Almost everyone has some knowledge of the various forms of leather and skin used for binding books. Calf and morocco are the most usual leathers used in modern times, and these may be treated by the tanner or the binder with various stains and polishes many of which have acquired technical names. Natural calf is one of the shades of light brown which the leather naturally assumes in the tanning process, and this is what you may expect to find if the binding is described as "calf" (or cf.) pure and simple. Calf can be stained to different colors and, especially since 1800, the range of colors has widened. Differential staining on calf is common from at least the beginning of the eighteenth century onwards. Thus you may find mottled or sprinkled calf, which describes the appearance produced by different treatments of the leather. Tree-calf is less self-explanatory. This was produced by a method of staining somewhat akin to the marbling of paper by which a pattern is produced that looks rather like a branching tree devoid of leaves. Such calf is usually very highly polished. From experience rather than from technical knowledge I should say that the method was first introduced towards the end of the eighteenth century. Spanish calf is stained in blotches of different colors, also rather like a primitive form of marbling. It is said to have originated in Spain and can be very effective and attractive.

Russia is calf treated in a special way. It is little used now because it does not wear well, but it was very popular from about 1730 to about 1850. It was prepared by treating skins with birch-bark oil which gives it its unmistakable smell. Sheepskin (abbreviated as "sheep," or even "shp.") resembles calf superficially, but takes a rather different hue in tanning. It also has distinctly poor wearing qualities.

Undressed, or rough, calf is simply calf with the skin reversed — that is, having the undressed side outwards. It has a sort of pile surface similar to the leather of suede shoes. "Divinity calf" is stained to a very dark brown shade, or even black, blind-stamped with no gilding. It is so-called because it was a style favored for binding theological works.

A technicality of binding terminology worth remembering is that a half-leather binding, unlike half-cloth, implies that not only the back, but also the outer corners of the book are covered with similar leather to that used for the back. Without these corners the correct description is "quarter"-leather. That is the strictly correct method, but quarter-leather is often called "half" in booksellers' catalogues, and it would be pernickety to cavil at this.

Morocco is made from the hide of goats and its generic name indicates the original home of the best kind of goatskin from which morocco for binding was procured. Levant morocco was also originally a goatskin of Levantine origin, but it is now more generally used to describe a method of treating skins to produce a grain of excellent wearing quality capable of taking a very high polish. Niger morocco is of broader grain and its quality is less consistent and less enduring than levant. These last two are often described as "levant" and "niger" without the addition of the word "morocco."

French morocco, on the other hand, was not necessarily produced from the hide of a native goat, but was treated by a process peculiar to French leatherworkers. Its individuality cannot easily be described in words, indeed experts sometimes differ as to the country of origin of old morocco. You must learn about this by experience, and it may help you to recognize French morocco when you see it if you familiarize yourself with the characteristic tools used by French binders. The preparation of leather for binding has achieved a very high standard in France throughout the last three hundred years.

Straight-grain morocco is a peculiarly English technique. It reached a high level in the first quarter of the nineteenth century and is particularly favored by collectors of the color-plate books of that period. (See pp. 161–2.) Its characteristic, long, straight, grained pattern gives it its name and, although there are imitations of it, you should easily recognize it when once it has been pointed out to you.

Every kind of skin, including human and reptilian, has been used for binding books, and one of the most lasting and effective is vellum (Old French, *vélin* – a calf), originally made exclusively from calfskin, though some of the purest and finest vellum has been produced for centuries from the skin of sheep. This was first used as a medium on which to write books, and this use of it antedates the form which books have acquired in modern times. When books were still written and preserved in the form of scrolls, vellum was being used as the basic material. This use for it is said to have been devised in the island of Pergamos when the ancient Egyptians prohibited the export of papyrus, on which books had previously been written. One name for vellum – parchment (German, *Pergament*) – commemorates this origin. This material should be carefully distinguished from Jap, Japon, or Japanese vellum, and also from vegetable parchment, all of which are synthetic products of inferior quality. A rough test for vellum is to lay the palm of your hand on it; if it is the real stuff it will feel very cold. A more dangerous test is to use a piece of indiarubber lightly on the surface; this is quite safe with real vellum, but will damage the imitations irreparably. The use of the words "vellum" and "parchment" in various compound expressions to describe artificial or synthetic materials is reprehensible, but probably too common to hope for its abandonment. This is a great pity, for the practice takes in vain the names of two ancient, venerable, and attractive materials and applies them to shams of the most doubtful nature. A professional bookbinder of high standing, in vigorous support of such a protest, writes to me: "Vellum is calf and parchment is sheepskin. . . . Vellum is really the most beautiful material a binder has at his disposal. . . . A binder who confused the terms and described his parchment as vellum could probably be proceeded against for misdescription." So much for the real thing: but it is almost more than deceptive; it approaches the fraudulent to foist upon us these substitutes which have none of the qualities of the originals save for a very superficial resemblance.

Vellum may be "limp," that is to say with a minimum of stiffening, which is an irritating form of binding, for nothing that I know of will prevent it from curling abominably; or it may be used to cover a stout board like any other skin, when its wearing qualities are unexceptionable. It is susceptible of attractive staining and takes stamping, whether blind, colored, or gilt, exceedingly well. Pigskin and roan (the latter a poor quality material made from sheepskin) are also used for binding, and it is a wartime discovery that ratskin has a very attractive appearance as the covering for a book.

Faults or defects in the binding are usually clearly indicated by the catalogue description. Such expressions as worn, rubbed, scored, joints weak, boards loose (i.e., sides detached from the spine) are more or less self-explanatory. "Binding copy" means that the covers at present on the book are in such poor condition as to make rebinding imperative. "Reading" (or "working") copy applied to a first edition is something worse: it probably means that, as a first edition, the book is valueless owing to its poor condition. Rebacking means that the spine has been renewed. This can be done exceptionally well; it can also be done exceedingly badly. I am often asked whether a rebacked copy is preferable to one in which the original backstrip is defective. I always reply that it depends on circumstances. If the rebacking has been well done, especially if it has been possible to retain the old back and to remount it carefully on the new spine, then unquestionably the repaired copy is preferable. Apart from the fact that you have been spared the sometimes not inconsiderable expense and delay of having the repairs undertaken, a binder never knows what trouble he may meet with in repairing old covers, and spines are almost as tricky to handle in books as they are in humans. Sometimes the old material is so dry and perishable that it flakes into nothingness as soon as it is lifted. Well-repaired copies of books are therefore greatly to be preferred to damaged ones, but repairs are defects—how serious depends entirely on the care and skill with which the repair has been effected.

Sometimes a leather binding is described as "extra,"

thus, you may find calf (or morocco) gilt extra. This is a bookbinding term which has been taken over by booksellers, and it had, originally, a definite technical meaning. Booksellers use it rather more loosely to describe any especially ornate binding, but a few words on what it originally meant to bookbinders may interest you and help you to understand what sort of thing the bookseller has in mind when he uses it in his catalogue.

Bookbinders speak of "half-extra," "extra," and "super-extra" and each of these has, or used to have, some special implication in the finishing of a book. "Finishing," by the way, is a technical term in bookbinding and the finisher is a most important and highly skilled craftsman. He is the man who takes over the volume after it has been folded, sewn, trimmed, and covered with leather and he adds all the finishing touches, whether these are simply the lettering on the back or the most elaborate ornamentation, stamping, and tooling.

When the finishing is "half-extra" the end-papers are usually of marble paper; on the inside of the book, where the edge of the leather is turned over and pasted down, there is ornamentation put on with a roll, similar to Numbers one and two in the illustration of bookbinders' tools, and a similar ornamentation is added to the sides as near to the edges as possible. These are usually tooled in blind.

"Extra" means that better marbled paper is used, the headband is of silk, and the rolls inside and outside are gilded. "Super-extra" calls for a full gilt back, the best marbles and the finest silk, a deeper inside roll and two rolls on each side, front and back. Between the two outside rolls, and anywhere else that took his fancy, the binder might have added any ornamentation that appealed to him, or that seemed to improve the appearance of the book. The spine will be fully gilt, with extensive ornamentation between the raised bands beneath which pass the cords that hold the book together. In other words, the description "extra" means just what it implies—something superior in the gilding or ornamentation of the binding.

A "*doublure*" means that the insides of the cover have been covered with leather. The description "silk *doublure*" is sometimes used, but this is technically incorrect; "inside *doublure*" is tautological because a *doublure* is never anywhere but inside the covers, replacing the end-papers, or rather covering them. It is said that Badier, a French binder, was responsible for this innovation in about 1703.

One of the earliest methods of binding books was to use stout wooden boards, usually of oak, for the sides with a strip of leather to hold them together and cover the spine. In the sixth century the monks of the Middle East began to cover these boards with metal, sometimes they used silver or gold and ornamented the sides with jewels. These are called Byzantine bindings or coatings and some of them are very impressive, although the method is quite alien to our notion of what should constitute the covering of books.

In the Middle Ages the practice arose of covering the heavy wooden boards with leather, usually pigskin, and of ornamenting the leather by chiseling, cutting, or tooling it. Gradually the boards became lighter and the preparation of different kinds of skin for the binder's use changed the aspect of the book externally, concurrent with the internal changes wrought by the introduction of printing and the eventual reduction in the sizes of books. The first books that were printed, as I have already mentioned, were large and cumbersome and heavy bindings of wooden boards were not unsuitable for them: but as printers came more and more to design books to be held in the hand rather than to lie on tables or lecterns, the binding had to be made to follow suit.

Certain styles of binding are closely associated with the names of their originators or chief exponents. Sometimes these were collectors like Jean Grolier whose books were usually bound in a very characteristic style with a geometrical pattern of strapwork, inlaid or painted in different colors. Grolier's books almost invariably bore his name and motto on their sides, but bookbinders occasionally used similar patterns for other patrons and booksellers usually describe these as "Grolieresque" bindings. Other styles are associated with the binders who designed them; thus you may see bindings described as in the style of Mearne or Roger Payne. No exhaustive account of these styles can be attempted here. Monographs on old bindings are nearly always expensive, because they cannot be satisfactorily undertaken without a great deal of illustration and elaborate description by an expert. Some of the best modern books on bindings are by G. D. Hobson and if you can get access to some of these you will see what a fascinating subject the history of old bindings can be.

But more than half our space is gone and we have not advanced beyond the covers and the title-page. New endpapers, lack of half-titles or errata leaves are annoying defects that should be mentioned in a catalogue. Recasing means that the book has been taken out of its covers and put back again, which is done when it is loose in the binding. This may entail resewing and the provision of new mull (see p. 60); the end-papers may be renewed and the strip of paper inside the hollow back of the book may also have been renewed. This is a very serious matter where modern books are concerned, and if the book is collected as a first edition, and the original binding is a consideration, such copies should be bought only with your eyes wide open and in the light of my remarks in Letter V. That is to say you should buy such copies only if the books are beyond your reach in pristine condition.

Letter IV was concerned with book sizes, but now that we are analyzing catalogue descriptions we must go a little further. Some booksellers do not concern themselves with the niceties of meaning of such terms as folio, quarto, and the rest. Strictly speaking, these are not indications of size at all, but many booksellers use them as such in their catalogues. They may be perfectly well aware of the bibliographical meaning of the terms, but they use them in their catalogues to convey to their customers the approximate sizes of the books described. Thus a folio in their catalogue means a large book, a 12mo a small one, and so on. This is not really at all satisfactory where rare books are concerned – it may even be actually misleading in some cases – but it is a rough-and-ready method suitable to the purpose they intend it to serve. We shall consider these terms, however, as what they really are, which is an indication of format rather than size; to gain even an approximate notion of the size of a book you need to know the size of the original sheet before it was folded. Fortunately, there is a convenient shorthand which gives this too. Thus, an "atlas" or an "elephant" folio means one printed on an exceptionally large sheet, and all books of this size are cumbersome. The size of the ordinary novel is crown octavo (abbr., cr. 8vo), which means that the sheet was of crown size and has been imposed and folded (see p. 64) to an octavo format. Crown sheets measure $15'' \times 20''$, and as one of them is folded three times to make an octavo you will readily see that the size of a page in crown octavo, *before it is trimmed*, is $7\frac{1}{2}'' \times 5''$.

Pocket editions in octavo, the page size of which is approximately $6\frac{3}{4}'' \times 4\frac{1}{4}''$, are imposed on a foolscap sheet, which measures $13\frac{1}{2}'' \times 17''$. Demy (pronounced "dem-eye," with the accent on the second syllable) is a sheet $17\frac{1}{2}'' \times 22\frac{1}{2}''$, and is commonly used for biographies, travel books, and other non-fictional works. The full page size is $8\frac{3}{4}'' \times 5\frac{5}{8}''$. Rarely used now, but frequently seen in bookseller's catalogues is "Roy." (i.e., Royal) 8vo, page size $10'' \times 6\frac{1}{4}''$.

Theoretically it would be possible to apply any of these qualifications to any format, which simply means that you could impose a folio on a sheet of crown size, or an octavo on an elephant sheet, but this is not done. What you should get clear in your mind is that the terms folio, quarto, etc., refer to the finished work, after it is folded, and the terms crown, elephant, etc., to the size of the sheet before it is folded.

Here is a list of the usual sizes of the unfolded sheets with their technical names, and if you are now fairly familiar with the details given in Letter IV you should be able to translate the booksellers' descriptions without much difficulty. There are other and curious sizes used in modern books, but these do not often occur in booksellers' catalogues, and they will not concern your book-collecting activities very much, if at all.

Name	*Abbreviation*	*Size of Sheet*
Atlas	Atl.	34″ × 26″
Elephant	El.	28″ × 23″
Imperial	Imp. or Impl.	30″ × 22″
Super Royal	Sup. or Roy.	27½″ × 20½″
Royal	Roy.	25″ × 20″
Medium	Med.	23″ × 18″
Demy	None	22½″ × 17½″
Crown	Cr.	20″ × 15″
Post	None	19¼″ × 15½″
Foolscap	F'cap	17″ × 13½″

If you are interested in working out the details of this you might provide yourself with sheets of paper cut to these sizes and, by folding them to various formats, arrive at the size of untrimmed pages.

All these technical names for sheet-sizes have a historical origin and, although modern methods of manufacture have largely superseded their applicability, I think they are sufficiently interesting to warrant a paragraph on the subject. Thus the smallest sheet of paper made had a watermark of a jug, or pot, and was called "pott," so that pott 8vo usually means a rather small book. The next size was watermarked with a cap and bells – hence "foolscap"; then came "post," with the watermark of a post horn; "crown," with a crown watermark, and so on. This nomenclature did not originate with the use of the watermarks themselves; all the watermarks I have mentioned were invariably used in sheets of a particular size long before they were used to indicate the size of the sheet. McKerrow, in his *Introduction to Bibliography*, says that when Prynne, the famous Puritan critic of the theater, complained that Shakespeare's plays were printed on the best crown paper, "far better than most Bibles," which he thought significant of the sinfulness of his age, he was referring not to the size, but to the quality of the paper. In other words, in Prynne's time, to describe any paper as "crown" meant that it was of very high quality and had no reference to the size of the paper used.

Dr. R. W. Chapman, however, in the *Library* (see p. 101), quotes a manuscript report made in 1674 to Bishop Fell, a great typographer, in which it seems that such terms as pott and the rest had already come to be used to denote paper sizes, although already at that date they were becoming obsolete because the special watermarks were no longer exclusively reserved for particular sizes.

The description of a book's edges may be important in the case of collected books. "Uncut" means, of course, that they are in the same state as they were when the book was issued, but if a book was issued with the edges trimmed the fact may not be mentioned in the catalogue, and the original condition of the book will be traceable only by its being in original binding. A shorthand description of the edges may be given by the use of certain initials. Thus t.e.g. means top edges gilded, and you may also get m.e. (marbled edges), y.e. (yellow edges), s.e. (sprinkled edges), and so on. A rebound copy of an old book may be described as "t.e.g. others uncut." Gauffered edges have impressions made in the gilding with binders' tools.

If a book is described as wholly or partially washed, that means that a part or all of the leaves were so badly stained that it has been given to a binder, who has taken it to pieces, washed it in some chemical bath, resized the paper to restore its original slight gloss, and then has put the book together again. This, as you will readily see, is a rather serious defect in a book, and you will soon come to recognize the unnatural whiteness of leaves that have been so treated, their ultra-crispness and, if it is a very bad case, the washed-out appearance of the ink of the type or illustrations.

Sometimes a very valuable and very old book that is imperfect may be made up in one of several ways. Perhaps two imperfect copies of a first edition are used to make one perfect one, and, if this is carefully done under the supervision of an expert, there is very little objection to it. Cause for objection arises, however, from the whole idea of tampering with books in this way. Unscrupulous persons will not hesitate to make up books from two different editions if they think they can get away with it, and it may be years before the unsuspecting buyer discovers the trick that has been played on him. The best protection you, as a beginner, have against trickery of this sort is to deal with a reliable bookseller who will point out to you any defects that he is aware of.

A book may be described as having some leaves from a smaller or shorter copy. (A "tall" copy is one with good margins, a "short" one the opposite). This means that some leaves are smaller than others, that is to say they have been taken from a copy that has suffered more severely at the hands of a binder. Usually these copies should be shunned. Before we leave the subject of size we had better consider the technical terms "cropped" and "shaved." These mean rather more than very small margins; if used with no qualification they usually mean that there has been some loss of printed matter. The cataloguer should specify how much, by saying that some numerals, or, in worse cases, headlines have been cut into. If the text has been partially cut away and he does not say so, he is a bad cataloguer, and if you find him persisting in such practices you had better steer clear of him. He may not be dishonest, but just careless; the results are the same for the reader of his catalogues. The amount of damage done by wormholes should also be specified. If these do not extend beyond the margins they are of comparatively little account, but if any part of the text is destroyed it is a different matter. Any good binder can repair wormholes and kill the worm if it is still active, but he cannot suply missing text except in facsimile.

This brings us to the question of leaves in facsimile. Missing leaves are usually, although not always, at the beginning or end of a book and are caused by wear and tear when the book has been left about without one or both of its covers. The missing parts may be supplied in various ways, sometimes by hand, varying all the way from a mere copy of the original text to a faithful replica so excellently performed on old paper that it would deceive all but the most expert. It may be in type, which would probably resemble the original only approximately, lithographed, or by some photographic process. None of these methods is more than a makeshift and all effect the value of the book very considerably. There is here, generally speaking, no question of deception. Our forefathers were not so particular about the condition of their books and were often quite content with an imperfect copy made up with facsimiles. The modern attitude towards them is that it is, on the whole, better to have a book with any missing material supplied in facsimile form than to leave it simply imperfect. It is largely a matter of taste and the length of one's purse. Moreover, these makeshifts in relation to imperfections, for makeshifts they are and rather sorry ones, are intolerable in books published after 1800, although they must sometimes be suffered in books prior to, say, 1600.

Catalogues vary enormously in the information they offer to the buyer. Generally speaking, the more information given the better, but printing is expensive and where catalogues consist very largely of cheap secondhand books it would be unreasonable to expect the same elaboration of descriptions as from catalogues consisting largely of high-priced rarities. Furthermore, if you expect your bookseller to be supplied and familiar with all the most expensive and authoritative works of reference on all the books he catalogues, you must be prepared to pay for it. The fact that some booksellers charge higher prices than others for similar books is partly because they have premises in expensive neighborhoods in order to be accessible to the bigger buyers, and partly because they have a staff of experts to catalogue their books at whose disposal they have placed an expensive reference library. You pay, therefore, for the confidence with which you may deal with them.

But there are certain things which any cataloguer worth his salt should include, and one of the most important of these is the date, when it is known. It may not be given anywhere in the book, in which the cataloguer may be able to ascertain the date exactly or approximately from a work of reference. In either case he will put it in square brackets, and if it is not exact he will preface the figures with the letters "ca.," or "c.," meaning circa, or he may say "n.d." (i.e., no date). A collection of pamphlets or books, each with a different date, may be described as "v.d." (various dates), "v.y." (various years).

Omissions are just as instructive to the expert as what is included in a description. Thus, if there is no mention of whether the edges of a book are trimmed or untrimmed it may be taken for granted that they are trimmed. On the other hand, if the collation (see pp. 66–70) of a perfect copy of a book calls for a half-title (see p. 60) and the lack of it is not mentioned, you are justified in supposing that it is present. The same applies to errata leaves and to any advertisements that really belong to the book and are not merely inserted at the end by the binder. It is, in fact, justifiable to assume that books described in a catalogue are perfect unless there is some statement to the contrary, even if the catlogue nowhere explicitly says that this is so; and any bookseller should accept the return of an imperfect book without question if it is sent back promptly with a note of the defect not mentioned in his description.

There is much more that might be said about reading a catalogue; I could write a whole book about it. Illustrations, title-pages, and so on may be "mounted" or "laid down," which means that they have been pasted to a piece of paper which is not part of the book because they needed strengthening in some way. If they are also "cut round" or "cut down," it means, of course, that they are smaller than the rest of the book and there is no guarantee that they belong to the particular copy in which they are found.

YOURS SINCERELY,

P. H. MUIR

LETTER EIGHT

A Short History of Book-Production

DEAR EVERYMAN:

IT is late in the day, and this is a very inadequate method for treating a subject so huge as the history of books. Even if I propose to confine myself to printed books, which I do not, it seems almost impious to attempt the subject in the space of even a fairly long letter. Nevertheless I am going to attempt it.

The earliest date that can be given for a printed book is the year A.D. 868, but book-printing did not enter the Western world for another six hundred years. In Europe it began about five hundred years ago. Twenty centuries before that the Assyrians made books by incising characters in soft clay and then baking the tablets in a kiln much in the way that bricks are made today. It is a long way from the widely circulated books of our time to such ancient and clumsy expedients.

Even if we could visit the first public library, opened in Rome in A.D. 39, we should hardly recognize it for what it was, for its "books" would be scrolls tied with tape, and it would look to us more like an enormous muniment room than a library.

During the third century of our era books first began to assume their modern form, consisting of leaves sewn together within covers so that they would stand on shelves.

You know, of course, that almost every invention affecting our cultural life originated in China. This wonderful, ancient civilization anticipated the Western world by the invention of paper (A.D. 105), printing ink (A.D. 400), and printing itself (A.D. 868). Before the Norman conquest of England books were already being printed from movable type in China.

The almost complete ignorance of Chinese civilization in Europe may be judged from the incredulity with which Marco Polo's accounts of it were received in the fourteenth century, and although the Arabs brought back the secret of papermaking from their conquest of Samarkand in the middle of the eighth century, it was nearly three hundred years before this spread to Europe by way of the Moorish conquest of Spain.

Printing was re-invented in Europe in complete ignorance of the Chinese invention. Indeed, it was not until this present century that Europeans were even aware of the early date at which the Chinese discovered the art.

Before the invention of printing, of course, all books were written by hand and the industry centered originally around the monasteries, almost the only centers of literacy. Here, in the security afforded by the monastic life and financed by the great wealth of the churches, the calligraphic and artistic abilities of monkish scribes rose to such a high level that their best work is not inferior to the great paintings of the old masters.

Sometimes their work was done purely to the glory of God, as when they wrote books for the enrichment of ecclesiastical libraries, and sometimes it was commissioned by princes and noblemen, and sometimes they worked for the humbler but necessary provision of service-books for the use of their congregations. These cheaper books were copied by groups of lesser scribes from an original and, perhaps, more elaborate and expensive book.

A few records of the actual costs of preparing some of these different kinds of manuscripts still survive. For instance, a missal which is still at Westminster Abbey was presented by an abbot in the fourteenth century. Its cost was something under one hundred fifty dollars. Three processionals made about the same time for St. George's Chapel at Windsor, cost about three dollars each. That is in the money of the time, which is rather difficult to translate into modern terms. The purchasing power of money at that time has been variously computed as between ten and forty times as much as it is today. You may get some notion of the cost of these books from the fact that the Westminster scribe was paid two shillings a week – say forty cents – (and board and room provided presumably), whereas the "commons" of another is reckoned at tenpence a week – say fifteen cents. So you will probably not exaggerate very much if you reckon the handsome Westminster missal as costing not much under two thousand dollars and the processionals at about twenty to twenty-five dollars apiece. Even the Psalter which King's College, Cambridge, bought in 1447 for three and eightpence – about five cents – might represent ten or twenty dollars in our money, and this was probably a secondhand purchase. A secondhand copy of a current edition of the Psalms today would probably find its way to the five-and-ten box.

The introduction of mass-production methods caused by the invention of printing did not, in all probability, affect the situation very much to begin with. In the first place, the early printers were strongly affected by current methods of book-production and, revolutionary though the process was, printers took the manuscript-book as their model and copied it as slavishly as they could. That sort of thing often happens with new inventions. Think of the way in which the designers of early motorcars copied the horse carriage. The early printers felt that the wider public to whom printed books would appeal would expect something very much like the handwritten books which they already knew.

Thus the natural conservatism of the human animal helped to make printed books more expensive than they need have been to begin with. For all the best books had pictures in them and, as the new invention had made no provision for supplying these by machinery, they had to be added by hand, and the same illuminators who ornamented manuscripts were the only people available to the printer. Now, of the £35, or one hundred fifty dollars, which the Westminster missal cost, £22 was paid to the illuminators of the capitals, so that one of the most expensive features of written books had also to be shouldered by printers.

Furthermore, even when this expensive method of illustrating was dispensed with, early printers had no need to work on a basis of strict relation to cost of manufacture. The difference between the actual cost of the mass-produced as compared with the handmade article must have been considerable and the printer will have been able to compete with the scribe while still making a handsome profit. You must remember, too, that the printer was dependent on readers for the sale of his product, and these were not too plentiful in those early days. Another cheapening was due to the printer's use of paper as against the more costly vellum used by the scribe. In 1467 a bishop wrote to the Pope that printing was estimated to have reduced the price of books by about one fifth.

One most important outcome of competition with the scribes was that the printer was kept on his toes in retaining a high standard of quality in his production, with the result that the best work of the early printers has never been surpassed and seldom equaled in later times.

When the "Brains Trust" on the English radio was asked to name inventions that had most affected the history of the human race, it struck me as odd that, although nearly all the members were authors, not one of them mentioned printing. And yet there are few inventions that have more radically affected the outlook and the daily lives of every one of us, and almost every invention since owes a great deal to printing, even if only for its publicity. Who was responsible for this major revolution which has so mightily affected the course of history? Strangely enough, his identity is not certainly known.

There are two main claimants to the honor, one a Dutchman called Coster, the other a German called Gutenberg. Modern scholarship has inclined heavily in favor of Gutenberg, and what has been called the Coster "legend" has been ridiculed. But very recent research suggests the possibility that Holland may have some sort of claim to the invention. Personally I see no reason why both claims should not be feasible. It would not be the only time when an important invention was perfected by more than one genius working independently. The almost simultaneous invention of the dynamo by Faraday in England and Henry in America is only one example of many.

However that may be, it is reasonably certain that at some time between 1440 and 1450 all the rather complicated essentials of a printing shop were sufficiently perfected to permit of small books being printed, bound, and distributed. The great revolution had begun and it was soon to advance by leaps and bounds. Before fifty years had passed most of the essential features of the printed book as we know it were already established and not merely the general appearance of books, but the means of producing them, remained unchanged in any important particular for more than three hundred years.

For example, by 1470 roman type had been perfected and would gradually make its way through nearly all western Europe. The French, it may be noted, never took kindly to the original Gothic or black letter type, and their printers used roman from the first.

Jenson designed the first perfect roman type and his is still one of the most elegant ever struck. When Cobden-Sanderson and Emery Walker started the Doves Press, about four and one half centuries later they had this type recast because they thought it had never been surpassed. Jenson was also the first non-German printer, if Coster's claim is disallowed. Jenson's edition of Pliny, printed in 1472, is one of the most noble monuments in the history of printing. Its current value is rather less than that of the Kelmscott Chaucer.

The year 1470 was a remarkable one. Not only was the modern type face perfected, but for the first time a page at the beginning of a book was set aside for nothing but the title and the date. Previously any such details that the printer designed to give were usually relegated to the end of the book to what is called the colophon, and this was often not easily distinguished from the end of the text. The title-page proper, as we know it, did not emerge for another six years – in a calendar printed in Venice.

In 1470, also, the leaves of a book were first numbered. This was in the same book which had the embryo title-page – an otherwise unexciting work, merely a sermon on the Feast of the Blessed Virgin. It has a preface by the author which may be the first appearance of such a thing in a printed book. Note that it was the leaves, not the pages of this book that were numbered. Pages were not numbered until 1499.

I have already mentioned the first form of book illustration. The cutting of wood-blocks, the earliest means of duplicating illustrations, cannot be certainly traced before 1423, and its first connection with books was in the making of what are now called block-books, so called because on each page the limited text is cut on the same wooden block from which the accompanying illustration was printed.

The most important feature of Gutenberg's invention was that each letter was cast separately and that the type could be distributed after use and be set up again to print different books. This process could be repeated until the face of the type became worn and defaced. Even then the metal could be melted down and recast in the original molds. But after the laborious process, possible only to an artist, of carving a set of blocks for a block-book, the resulting blocks could be used to print only that one book. It was the mobility of Gutenberg's invention that made it so important and that is why he is called the inventor of *movable* type.

In 1473 music appeared in a printed book for the first time. This is not quite true, for in 1457, at Mainz, Gutenberg's whilom partners included music in a Psalter, which was also the first book with a colophon. Three of the four staves in this book were printed, the fourth and the notes themselves being inserted by hand. This book also had printed initial letters instead of having them added by an illuminator—a very early attempt to dispense with this very expensive person. It may be mentioned here that calligraphers and scribes have a great place in the history of printing, for many fine types are based on their beautiful handwriting.

Even in 1473 the method of printing music was a laborious one, for the music staves had still to be ruled by hand and the notes put in by reversing type letters and printing the butts of them. Thus the notes were square, and not round as we know them, and they had no tails. You can see at once that the possibilities were extremely limited. I have no space to enter in detail into the history of music-printing, but to say that in 1476 an entire composition was cut on and printed from wood-blocks; movable type was used for music in Higden's *Polycronicon*, printed by Caxton's successor, de Worde, in 1495, but not perfected until the eighteenth century; and round heads for music were first used in 1532.

But we are running ahead of the calendar. At first, books were large and far from easy to handle. There were various reasons for this. Type faces were rather large, margins were wide, and such masterpieces of printing as the Mazarin Bible (so called because the book was first dated from a copy in Cardinal Marazin's library) and Jenson's lovely Pliny, are unhandy folios of considerable size and weight. One of the main requirements for the design of small books was a legible type of small size. It was reserved for one of the major figures in the whole history of printing to effect this revolution completely. This was Aldus Manutius, invariably referred to by his given name, whose artistry and craftsmanship first gave us books comfortable to hold in the hand, yet beautifully printed in legible type.

Aldus was a great printer and a notable scholar. I wish space would permit me more than a passing reference to his achievements, but you may read of them more fully in, for example, Orcutt's *Master Makers of the Book*. In 1499 he produced one of the handsomest illustrated books ever printed—Colonna's *Hypnerotomachia Poliphili*—the beautiful Poliphilus type commemorates it.

He was probably already at work then on the design of a type which would reduce the size and cheapen the price of books without sacrificing the highest standards of production. His type was based on calligraphic models of earlier date, and in 1501 he produced editions of Virgil and Juvenal that are twin monuments in the hierarchy of book production. Aldus had begun to produce the first books suitable for armchair reading. His type is called italic, a name which still commemorates its Italian origin.

William Caxton introduced printing into England. He

learned his trade at Cologne and helped to print a book there in 1472. In 1476 he began printing at Westminster, and was very soon producing an average of ten books a year. Although several of them were rather small, this was a considerable achievement. He was a scholar, translating into English many of the books that he printed, and even if his craftsmanship was not on the highest level, our debt to him is as obvious as it is enormous. He it was who first printed Chaucer, and he circumvented the official ban on printing the Bible in English by translating de Voragine's *Golden Legend*, and adding to it so considerably that the book includes almost the whole of the Old Testament and a great deal of the New Testament. This was probably his greatest achievement, and it may amuse you to know that the Earl of Arundel was so pleased with the book that he rewarded Caxton with an annual present of two deer—a doe in winter and a buck in summer.

Wynkyn de Worde, Caxton's successor, came from Alsace. In 1495-6 he printed the first book on paper made in England. It came from a paper mill in Herefordshire, which began production in 1494.

Neither Caxton nor de Worde was in the first flight as a printer. Their work is not in the same class as the best Continental printing of the time. Richard Pynson, a Norman, first started in London as a book distributor, but he eventually became a printer, and he was the first in England to pay much attention to the quality of the work he produced. He introduced roman type and acquired wood-blocks by artists from Continental printers because there were few good engravers in England. He was official printer to Henry VIII, and in 1521 he printed the attack on Luther which earned for Henry the Papal title of

"Defender of the Faith." Thomas Berthelet, who succeeded Pynson as Royal Printer, and John Day, whose device was the sun with the motto – "Arise, for it is Day" – produced some of the most beautiful books ever printed in England.

I have already mentioned the block-books which were entirely the work of wood cutters. The marriage of wood-blocks to movable type occurred in 1461, in the shop of Pfister at Bamberg. He seems to have been a woodcutter himself, and this may to some extent explain not only the considerable gap between the discovery of wood-blocks and their use in printed books, but also the continued appearance of block-books long after movable type was invented.

One difficulty was that if wood-blocks were to be printed side by side with type they had to be uniformly of the same height as the type metal, but this was a minor consideration compared with the restrictive methods used by the woodcutters themselves. Even before the invention of printing a guild of woodcutters was strong enough to prevent the use by book-printers of any cuts not made by a member of the guild. Pfister probably overcame this obstacle by being himself a member of the mystery. In any case, he gave book illustrations a great fillip.

Engraving on copper, which was known in Germany before the middle of the fifteenth century, was first used to illustrate a book at Bruges in 1476, by Mansion, Caxton's first master. This, like other early books illustrated in this way, does not always have the illustrations, and we know that they were not printed at the same time as the text. The plates were printed on a separate press and pasted into spaces reserved for them. Some copies of the book do not even make provision for the plates, others have spaces for only one, some for nine, and some for ten plates.

Beltini's *Monte Santo di Dio*, Florence, 1477, contains three copper engravings, but not until 1481, in a Florence edition of Dante's *Commedia*, do we find copper-engraving properly used for book illustration. Very few of the remaining copies of this book have all the nineteen plates engraved for it by Baldini from the designs of Botticelli. In most of them, many plate spaces are mere blanks.

Woodcutting, however, was the more favored process and many fine and elaborate books were illustrated by this means before the end of the fifteenth century. Dürer and his contemporaries illustrated some of the finest, but Aldus printed the finest of all.

Pynson was by no means the first to buy or borrow blocks from colleagues. The interchange of material by this and other more questionable means was extensive. You will find an excellent illustrated account of it in Pollard's *Old Picture Books*. You may be surprised to learn that color-printing was already used in the famous 1457 Psalter mentioned on p. 151. Ratdolt made extensive use of color in an astronomical work that he printed in Venice in 1485. He probably used stencils for his diagrams, but the nearest approach to a colored book illustration in this period was made by an unknown schoolmaster who printed the so-called *Book of St. Albans* in 1486. As many as three different colors are used in printing some of the heraldic shields in this book, but it is interesting to learn that yellow was always added by hand.

No other printer attempted colored book illustrations in England for two hundred years, when Le Blon, a Frenchman, introduced his process based on a study of Newton's scientific analysis of light. In every essential feature except the use of the camera, Le Blon anticipated all the modern methods of color reproduction.

The details of book illustration and other typographical innovations must be neglected here, but you may read of them elsewhere. One of the best general works on illustration is Burch's *Colour Printers*, which is a very valuable historical treatise and well illustrated.

We must push on to later centuries, but you see that within fifty years of the invention of printing itself all the essential features of book manufacture were already in common use. The general details of the methods used by the early printers are well described by McKerrow (see pp. 109–11).

The sixteenth century has many famous names in printing history. Geoffrey Tory designed beautiful books in France and introduced the accents and the cedilla, which every French student knows, as well as the apostrophe. The Netherlands became famous as a book-producing country when the Elzevir family began to issue pocket volumes and when Christopher Plantin began to print there in 1555. The firm he founded continued under the same name for more than three centuries.

Garamond designed his famous types; the New Testament was first printed in English; the first printing press on the American continent was set up in Mexico; handwriting began to be taught by means of copy-books; the Book of Common Prayer was first printed; the first metal screw for use in a printing press was devised; the first anthology of English poetry and the first blank verse were printed; printers began to use different letters for I and J and U and

V; the first bookseller's catalogue was issued; in Holland the first auction sale of books was held; and the first illustrated school-book was published before the end of the sixteenth century.

In the seventeenth century came the great Authorized Version of the Bible in 1611; John Minsheu was the first author to publish a book by subscription, and his *Guide into Tongues*, 1617, was the first book to print a list of subscribers; Blaeu introduced a method of springing the plate that presses inked type on to paper (i.e., the platen), a great labor-saving device. Star Chamber cast a dark shadow over the freedom of the press in England, and Milton wrote his courageous attack on censorship. Daye began the first press in North America; raised letters were suggested for teaching the blind to read; and Granjon and Fell produced famous type designs.

But the greatest revolution in book history in the seventeenth century, the one entirely new feature that was to affect it fundamentally, was the emergence of the publisher. The story must be almost dangerously oversimplified here. It begins with the first scribes, who prepared not only their own writing materials, pens, ink, pigments, and the rest, but the very skins on which they wrote. Gradually differentiation and specialization developed with the eventual result that an entrepreneur, who was nothing but a merchant, undertook the commissioning of the various tasks and the financial risk, and marketed the book as a finished article at a price fixed by himself. This was the stationer, the embryo of the publisher. In the days of written books he carried very little stock.

New elements emerged with the invention of printing, but generally speaking, the printers of the fifteenth century were in a fair way to becoming publishers much as we know them today.

In the sixteenth century printing tended to become divorced from publishing and the form of imprint—"Printed by John Doe for Richard Roe"—became common. Emphasis, on the whole, remained with the printer, who usually retained the right to sell copies of the books he printed by retail, and probably at least shared the risks and expenses of publication with the bookseller. But people who were booksellers pure and simple began to emerge. These booksellers co-operated with each other in assuming the risk of expensive publications. In 1623 four of them clubbed together to finance the first collected edition of Shakespeare's plays. This method developed, and in the eighteenth century as many as fifty or more booksellers sometimes joined hands in publishing important books.

The assumption by a single individual of financial responsibility in the publication of a book and the striking of a bargain between that individual and the author marks the birth of modern publishing. We may conveniently take Jacob Tonson and his dealings with Dryden as the prototype of such transactions. So that when, in 1679, Tonson borrowed £20 from another bookseller with which to purchase the publishing rights of Dryden's *Troilus and Cressida*, one of the earliest of modern publishing transactions may be said to have occurred.

The relations between authors and publishers were uncertainly based: any shadow of the now well-established notion of copyright was almost unknown. Piracy flourished almost unchecked, and a playwright was thought to behave shabbily if he reserved publication rights when selling a play to a producer.

Tonson's relations with Dryden, while not absolutely the first of the kind, were certainly among the earliest examples of long-standing association between a publisher and an author, and they mark very clearly the beginnings of a new standing for authors. Almost throughout the eighteenth century authors would still be dependent very largely on patronage, private or official, and those who could not secure it would be condemned to hack work like Goldsmith. Dr. Johnson was a brilliant exception. Like Beethoven in music, he was among the first to earn a living by his pen. Dryden, of course, was a successful playwright, but in his early days he is said to have done hack work for Herringman.

We obviously cannot follow this fascinating subject in any detail. It is too vast, but you may like to pursue it a little further in such books as those of Collins mentioned on p. 27, and in Mumby's *Publishing and Bookselling*, published in 1930.

The eighteenth century is remarkable for the books illustrated with copperplates in which the French school of illustration reached one of its peaks. Frenchmen were to use the wood-engraving and the lithograph—even the steel-engraving—to better purpose in the nineteenth century, but in the eighteenth century the picture book first gained a prominence which it has never lost.

This century was one of great culture throughout Europe. In England the Augustan Age in literature was accompanied by a great revival of interest in type and book design, and the general level of craftsmanship in book-production was extremely high. Such names as Caslon and

Baskerville, Horace Walpole and Roger Payne, have already been mentioned, but even ordinary commercial printers and binders, those who worked not especially for the connoisseur, but for the ordinary book-buyer, produced volumes pleasant to see and handle.

But it was in France that self-consciously fine work reached the highest levels. Typographers like Didot and Fournier, binders like Derôme and Padeloup, working with artists like Boucher and Moreau combined to design books not only the equal of books in any other period, but books that struck an entirely new note. It was an age of great riches and of great connoisseurship, also of great enterprise in all the arts.

English contributions in this particular field were neither numerous nor specially notable. English books were illustrated in the French manner, some of them were illustrated by French artists, but, in the main, English artists and publishers took an individual line of their own. The Bickham family, although their work is not usually on the highest artistic levels, are very representative of this English movement. These three engravers used the calligraphic method as their individual contribution to the illustration of books. The copy-book method of teaching handwriting was initially largely commercial. The great increase in international trade in the sixteenth and seventeenth centuries vastly widened the opportunities of a commercial career for those who could write and cipher.

Gradually, with the spread of literacy, calligraphy became also an elegant pastime for ladies and gentlemen who had no need to earn their bread and butter.

The Bickhams exploited this fashionable interest in calligraphy, first by the production of small copy-books, then in conjunction with music and vignette illustrations —*The Musical Entertainer*, 1736–9—and finally in *The Universal Penman*, 1731–43, the writing-book to end all writing-books. These books of the Bickhams are a peculiarly English development, and they have no counterpart in any other country that I know of.

Strikingly individual contributions to book illustration came from Hogarth in the first half of the century, notably with his plates for Butler's *Hudibras* in 1726, and from Blake in the second half—*Songs of Innocence*, 1789; *Songs of Experience*, 1794; *America*, 1793; *Jerusalem*, 1804, etc. But there was one medium of book illustration invented in the eighteenth century which was exploited more fully by British artists than by those of any other nation. This was the aquatint process.

It is said to have been invented by Le Prince, who exhibited his first plates in Paris in 1769, but, although fine books were illustrated by this process in France and Germany, it was used more extensively in England than anywhere. There are many successful aquatinters—Paul Sandby, who introduced the method into England; Havell, Stadler, Westall, Cruikshank, Alken, and many others—but it is curious that the name that stands out above all others in this connection—Thomas Rowlandson —was probably not himself an aquatinter, although most of his book illustration is reproduced by aquatint. From the figures in Ackermann's *Microcosm of London* to the comic plates in the *Tours of Dr. Syntax*, from his edition of *The Vicar of Wakefield* to the inimitable series satirizing Boswell, there is nothing in the whole course of English book illustration to match him. Much has been written about him but, for the best introduction to the work of a still underestimated master, you could not do better than read the chapters on him in Desmond Coke's *Incurable Collector*, itself a delightful book, and a charming memorial to a great collector of our own day.

In the embellishment of fine books, besides Roger Payne, there was Edwards of Halifax, whose individual style of binding is quite unmistakable. He used calf, seldom morocco, but he liked best to bind in vellum. He invented a method of rendering the vellum transparent so that he could paint pictures in reverse on the under side of the skin before binding the book. This, of course, preserved the paintings, and specimens of them are still found with these pictures in beautifully fresh condition.

He was also a prolific and able exponent of the fore edge painting. This was done by fanning out the gilded fore edge of a book, clamping it in a press, and painting a picture on it. When the paint was dry and the book was allowed to resume its original position, the painting was concealed by the gilding. This method is employed to perfection by modern artists, and it is seldom wise to buy a reputedly old fore edge painting without a pedigree—and not always then.

I have reproduced, in the group illustrations an example of Edwards's binding showing the fore edge painting. The pictures on the sides are after Sir Joshua Reynolds, the coronet on the spine and the initials are those of the Fitzroy family, and the fore edge painting is of Euston Hall. On the fly-leaf is a pedigree written by various members of the family, beginning with the original owner in 1785.

There were important developments in printing in America in the eighteenth century, most of them associated with the name of William Bradford. This remarkable man "printed the first New York paper currency (May 31, 1709), the first American Book of Common Prayer (1710), the first drama written in English America (1714), the first history of New York (1727), and the first copperplate plan of New York (Lyne's survey undated, but 1730)." The quotation is from the *Dictionary of American Biography* but much information about Bradford and the early history of printing in English America is contained in a most readable and reliable book by John T. Winterich: *Early American Books and Printing* (Houghton Mifflin, 1935, $2.50).

There you may read of Benjamin Franklin's career as a printer, of the first American newspapers—of the earliest of all, *Publick Occurences*, only one issue, September 25, 1690, was printed and only one single copy has survived, which is in the Public Record Office in London—of the history of the American magazine, and of much more in this fascinating but comparatively little-explored channel of American history.

Here are a few important dates in the eighteenth century: 1719, Réaumur suggested making paper from wood; 1722, Le Blon published *Coloritto*, an account of his method of color-printing, with nine specimens of his work; Walsh, the English music-publisher began punching pewter plates for music-printing—an enormous saving on the previous method of engraving, and one in use to this day; 1734, Caslon issued his first sheet of type specimens; 1739, Ged perfected stereotyping; 1744, Sotheby's auction rooms opened, the first in England devoted solely to the sale of books; 1754, Breitkopf perfected the first successful printing of music from movable type; 1757,

Baskerville's type designs published, Horace Walpole's private press started; 1768, Bodini started printing at Parma, first parts of the *Encyclopædia Britannica* published; 1769, Granger's *Biographical History of England* began the craze for extra-illustrating books which has continued to this day; about 1770 Roger Payne began binding; 1774, Scheele invented a process with a chlorine base for bleaching rags for papermaking; 1784, Haüy printed the first book in raised type for the blind; 1796, Senefelder invented lithography—a great epoch in book-production; 1797, Bewick's *British Birds* marked a revival of wood-engraving as a method of book illustration; 1800, Earl Stanhope perfected the first successful printing press made entirely of metal, and Koops, a Dutchman, printed a book on paper made from straw, the first successful attempt to produce book-paper without a rag basis, and one which was revived in England during the war due to acute shortages of raw materials.

It was in the nineteenth century, however, that the entire face of book-printing and -publishing was changed. The century was one of revolutionary mechanical advances of every kind. In the year 1800 a craftsman from the earliest cradle of printing in Mainz would have found as few fundamental changes in the printing shops as in the domestic amenities of the period. His house might be slightly better lit and slightly warmer, transport would be slightly smoother and quicker, the costumes would be unfamiliar, but in a few weeks or months the surprises would be exhausted. In the workshop, composition, imposition, inking, feeding, pressing, and the rest would be all a little more slickly accomplished, but the innovations would be easy for him to grasp. They would be all fairly simple adaptations and extensions of machinery with which he was perfectly familiar, and he would very soon find himself completely at home, and even a little more comfortable in a period three hundred and fifty years later than his own.

The next fifty years would see great changes, and another fifty still would see printing, binding, and publishing revolutionized so fundamentally in all their phases that this time our traveler would be at a disadvantage compared with a mechanically minded schoolboy with no knowledge of the mystery of printing, but with a good grasp of the fundamentals of mechanics.

Our craftsman would start in the composing shop, where mechanical composition, invented in 1822 and perfected in 1886, would be quite incomprehensible to him. The type-setting machine, a miniature type foundry actually manufacturing type from molten metal at the same time as it sets up the text of a book and justifies the lines and spaces as it does so, is still a major miracle to me, who have seen it at work a hundred times. What would it be to him, who thought himself master of every phase of printing!

The fast rotary presses, founded on the invention of König, first used for printing the *Times* in 1814, and perfected by Hoe in 1856, would bear no shadow of resemblance to the presses he knew in Mainz. The texture and feel of the paper would be completely unfamiliar to him. If it were a high quality book paper it would contain elements of esparto grass, first introduced by Routledge in 1861, but it might be cheap newsprint, made from chemical wood pulp, first successfully manufactured in Sweden by Ekman in 1874, and this he might hardly recognize as paper at all, so different would it appear from the superb handmade material which was the only paper he knew.

If the books he saw printed were illustrated they might contain line-blocks, invented by Gillot in 1859, whose son, in 1872, applied photography to the method; or they might be half-tones, perfected by a multiplicity of experimenters in the 1880's. Remember, too, that the photographic basis of these illustrations—invented in 1839—would also be a miracle of unfamiliarity to him. A very high-class book might contain collotype illustrations at any time after 1865, when the method was made practical by two inventors in Metz.

One thing would reassure him. The organization of workers in a printing office into "chapels" is as old as printing itself, and many ancient trade customs are still preserved in the most modern printing works.

The astonishments that would await him in the binder's shop must not detain us here. Sufficient to say that folding, gathering, sewing, and casing would all be done by machines before his amazed eyes, and the material in which the books were bound would itself puzzle him beyond measure. While he is still gasping at the revolutions effected since his last halt in time one hundred years earlier, let us transport him to a publisher's office.

Modern conceptions of publishing as an organization entirely divorced from printing might not be entirely new to him. You may remember that Pynson was a publisher before he was a printer. But the details and organization of modern publishing would be no less unfamiliar to him than to any eighteenth-century companion who might have joined him on the last hop of his time-machine.

For in the interval publishers had not merely abandoned the keeping of retail bookshops where they sold books issued by other publishers as well as their own (a few anachronistic examples of this still survive); not only would the scale and tempo of the publisher's office astonish him, but, if he inquired at all closely into its methods, he would find them very strange and bewildering.

"Copyright" would be a word that he might have picked up in 1800, but he would have found it hard then to decide whether the *right* of making *copies* (i.e., copyright) was vested in the author or the bookseller, and which of the two the law was concerned to protect. Certainly all through the eighteenth century law cases abound in which the booksellers sought "protection" against authors.

In 1709 the famous Act of Queen Anne was passed, by relying upon which a bookseller named Eyre in 1735 successfully claimed perpetual copyright to *The Whole Duty of Man*, first published in 1657; and in 1739 Tonson similarly acquired rights to *Paradise Lost*, first published in 1667. Even more remarkable was the judgment in 1768 which secured to Millar perpetual copyright to Thomson's *Seasons*. It is necessary to note that these actions were taken against other, pirating booksellers—the descendants of the authors were deemed to have no concern in the matter.

It is true that, by the end of the century the *legal* position was clarified, and authors were in some sense secured in their rights. But, on the one hand, pirates were busy in Dublin, undercutting the original publishers and by no means confining their activities to Ireland: and, on the other hand, it was customary for publishers to purchase the author's copyright outright for a single cash payment.

Sometimes this payment was for an edition of a specified number of copies, and further payments were made for reprints. Instances are on record, also, where publishers made further substantial payments to an author when the subsequent success of a book made the initial payment appear paltry. But such payments were *ex gratia;* the publisher was under no kind of obligation to make them. A successful author with an honest publisher might emulate Macaulay with his £20,000 for the *History of England*, but poor wretches like Clare might have to submit to profits being divided between the publisher and a third party who had secured this right by advancing the impecunious poet £20 before the publication of his book.

Authors had no control over or right to inspect the publisher's accounts, and many instances could be cited where advantage was taken of this fact to evade the terms of an agreement too favorable to an author.

Sir Walter Besant, himself a successful novelist, was among the first to tackle adequately the position of authors in their relations with publishers. He founded the Authors' Society in 1883, with the object of improving the position of authors in respect to copyright and to establish their right to a fair return for their labors with authority to examine or to have audited the accounts of sales furnished by the publishers.

At about this time, too, the author's agent came into being, acting on a commission basis and controlling the terms of agreements, especially in respect to the newly devised system of paying royalties in proportion to sales, which quickly ousted the less satisfactory method of paying a fixed sum for publication rights.

1894, Ashendene Press founded, the *Yellow Book* began publication with Beardsley as art editor, the "Beardsley Period" was at its peak and a new school of book illustration thus began; 1895, the publication of *Pan* marked the beginning of the modern German revival of fine typography; 1896, Ricketts and Shannon founded the Vale Press, which printed no books itself, but designed fine books to be commercially printed; 1900, Cobden-Sanderson founded the Doves Press.

Thus were laid the foundations of modern book-production in the nineteenth century. There is little fundamental that has been added since. There has been a great revival of temporarily neglected type faces and methods of production. The work of pioneers like Morris, St. John Hornby, and Cobden-Sanderson has profoundly affected publishing and commercial printing in the right direction, and machine-setting has been adapted to do fine work fairly comparable with hand-setting. Engraving, on both metal and wood has been re-introduced as a means of illustrating fine books. Francis Meynell has revived the traditions of Pickering and Ricketts by publishing at the Nonesuch Press books planned by a talented designer carried out by commercial printers under his direction. The limited edition revives memories of Horace Walpole and a love for the past brings things full circle to the anachronistic survival of hand-presses, whose work is often not the equal of the best mechanical products.

Here I must end this headlong rush through the centuries. I regret its inadequacies, but I have deliberately underlined the beginning and end of the period in the hope that you may grasp their vital importance incomparably beyond and above all other periods of printing history. I have tried to show you that the first fifty years of printing established all the essentials of the craft, that the ensuing three hundred years or so were spent in perfecting and developing the potentialities of the invention, and that the last hundred years or so have revolutionized it out of all knowledge. Probably little remains to be done to the book as we know it beyond the perfection of detail.

The half-tone method by which the illustrations in this book are printed, and which entails the use of shiny paper, was already on the way out before the war. It will be replaced by some process that eliminates the intermediate step between the photograph and the printed page which is the half-tone block itself. Collotype, or some equally inoffensive development of photography, is probably the answer. A method that reproduces in the illustration almost every feature of the original photograph, dispensing with the makeshift of the screen-and-dot method essential to the half-tone process, and with the horrid sheen of "art" paper which destroys the homogeneity of a book, is to be desired.

Is there any future beyond that? Will the reading matter of the future resemble our printed books as little as they resemble the clay tablets of the Assyrians? Probably, and if so, it will be along the lines of greater portability and cheapness. These two things have dominated the evolution of books since the beginning, and it would be idle to suggest that the limits of that evolution have been reached.

The flood of inventiveness that is already flowing will not leave books as they are. I will venture few predictions except to suggest that in the future books will remain largely visual. There is, in my opinion, no general future for the talking book. It may be, of course, that a new kind of conditioned reflex will arise as a result of broadcasting. More and more people seem to find a radio background essential to their daily lives. In many households the radio is switched on all day. People tend increasingly to overhear rather than to listen to radio programs. The housewife welcomes music while she works, and may equally welcome the reading aloud of a novel while she knits or sews—with headphones, we may hope. It may be, therefore, that a cheap method of supplying talking books with a circulating library as the obvious method of distributing the records will find a larger audience than I anticipate.

But such a method would obviously supplement rather than supplant the printed book. It is much more likely that some development of photography will supplant typography in the production of at any rate some kinds of books. An extension of the use of microfilm with a simple miniature form of illumination, coupled with a magnifier and perhaps a "proto-book" on to the blank pages of which the miniature slides would be projected may be already on the way.

On the brink of such horrors I take my leave of you, my dear Everyman, to plunge nostalgically into the pleasant waters of the past.

However, before taking leave of you, dear Everyman, —temporarily, I hope, for the reception of this book has determined me to write a sequel to it—I wish you well. It has been necessary, by the nature of the task, to dwell overmuch on the difficulties of book-collecting and they have assumed a disproportionate measure of attention. The pleasures easily outweigh them and if I have been the means of injecting into your veins the insidious but pleasant collecting virus I hope you will think that I have done well by you.

Nevertheless it would not be fair to leave you thus, with the pleasant impatience of anticipation urging you to get going. Pause and reflect before you take the first step, for it is an irrevocable one: once you have taken it you will never be the same man again. This new interest will become more absorbing, its appetite grows with feeding, and once you enter the company of bibliophiles you will be committed for life. I hope you may be—there is no better service that I could do to any man than to induct him into such a company; but if this book has done it for you then at least I feel you have embarked with your eyes fairly wide open.

YOURS SINCERELY,

P. H. MUIR

A SHORT LIST OF ABBREVIATIONS COMMONLY USED IN CATALOGUES

A.D. —— *Autograph document. (Note the difference between A.D. and A.L.S., A.L. and A.L.S. on the one hand, and D.S. and L.S. on the other. The S. means that the document, note, or letter is signed by the writer; the A. means that the body of the letter is in the handwriting of the signatory.)*

A.D.S. —— *Autograph document signed.*

A.L. —— *Autograph letter.*

A.L.S. —— *Autograph letter, signed.*

A.N.S. —— *Autograph note, signed.*

ANON. —— *Anonymous.*

B.L. —— *Black letter (i.e., printed in Old English characters).*

B.D. or BND. —— *Bound.*

BDG. —— *Binding.*

BDS. —— *Boards.*

BROWNED. —— *Stained or discolored by age.*

C. or CA. —— *Circa.*

CENT. —— *Century.*

CF. —— *Calf.*

CL. —— *Cloth.*

CL. BDS. —— *Cloth boards.*

COL. or COLD. or CLD. —— *Colored.*

CONT. or CONTEMP. —— *Contemporary.*

CP. or CF. —— *Compare.*

CR. —— *Crown.*

CUTS. —— *Wood-cuts.*

D. or DOC. —— *Document.*

D.W. or D/W. —— *Dust wrapper.*

E.D.L. —— *Edition de luxe.*

ED. or EDIT. —— *Edited or editor.*

ED. or EDN. —— *Edition.*

EL. —— *Elephant.*

ENG. or ENGR.—*Engraved or engraving.*
EX. or EXT.—*Extra.*
EX-LIB.—*Ex-library (i.e., with labels on or removed from covers).*
F.—*Folio (i.e., leaf).*
FAC., FACS. or FACSIM. *Facsimile.*
FCAP. or FCP.—*Foolscap.*
FF.—*Folios (i.e., leaves).*
FO. or FOL.—*Folio.*
FRONT.—*Frontispiece.*
G.—*Gilt.*
G.E.—*Gilt edges.*
G.L.—*Gothic letter (printed in Gothic type).*
G.T.—*Gilt top.*
H.M.P.—*Hand-made paper.*
HF.—*Half (e.g., hf. cf., hf. mor., etc.).*
ILL.(S.)—*Illustration(s).*
ILLUS.—*Illustration or illustrated.*
IMP.—*Imperial.*
INTROD.—*Introduction.*
ITAL.—*Italics.*
JUV.—*Juvenile.*
L.P.—*Large paper.*
L.S.—*Letter signed.*
M.E.—*Marbled edges.*
MOR.—*Morocco.*
MS., MSS.—*Manuscript(s).*
N.D.—*No date.*
N.P.—*No place, or no publisher.*
OB. or OBL.—*Oblong.*
ORIG.—*Original.*
P., PP.—*Page(s).*
P. 8VO. or P. 8°.—*Post octavo.*
PARCH.—*Parchment.*
PICT.—*Pictorial.*
POL.—*Polished.*
PORT.—*Portrait.*

P.P.——*Privately printed.*
PRES.——*Presentation.*
REV.——*Revised.*
RUS. or RUSS.——*Russia.*
S.A.——Sine anno (*undated*).
S.A.L.——et n. Sine anno, loco, et nomine. *Without date, place, or name of printer or publisher.*
SHP.——*Sheep.*
SIG.——*Signature.*
S.L.——Sine loco.
SM.——*Small.*
S.N.——Sine nomine.
S.P.——*Small paper.*
SPR.——*Sprinkled.*
SQ.——*Square.*
ST.——*Stitched.*
SUBS.——*Subscriber or subscription.*
SUP.——*Super.*
SWD.——*Sewed.*
T.E.——*Top edges.*
THK.——*Thick.*
T.P.——*Title page.*
UNB. or UNBD.——*Unbound.*
V.D.——*Various dates.*
V.Y.——*Various years.*
VEL. or VELL.——*Vellum.*
VIGN.——*Vignette.*
VOL.——*Volume.*
W.A.F.——*With all faults* (*i.e., not returnable*).
Y.E.——*Yellow edges.*

A LIST OF BOOKS FOR FURTHER READING THAT HAVE BEEN RECOMMENDED IN THESE PAGES

(The dates, publishers, and published prices have been added whenever possible. Many of the books are permanently or temporarily out of print and the original prices have been added as some guidance to the seeker for secondhand copies.)

ALDIS, Henry G.: *The Printed Book*, second edition, revised by John Carter and E. A. Crutchley (Macmillan, 1941, $1.75).

AMES, J.: *Typographical Antiquities.* 1749. Another edition, enlarged by W. Herbert, 4 vols., 1785–90. Another edition, edited by T. F. Dibdin, 4 vols. 1810–19. (Note – Dibdin's edition was not completed. It supersedes Herbert as far as it goes. The recommendation of the book in my text has a double purpose; for the collector of printing and publishing styles the 1749 edition is the important one, because it was the first to abandon the long "s"; Herbert's and Dibdin's editions are better for reference purposes, as they are so much fuller.)

BESTERMAN, Theodore: *World Bibliography of Bibliographies* (2 vols., $30.00 each). (Note – worth consulting, but not worth buying. Is in course of being revised and enlarged.)

BURCH, R. M.: *Colour Printing* (Pitman, 1910).

The Cambridge History of English Literature (15 vols., Macmillan, 1931, $25.00). (Note – The student for whom fifteen volumes sound too formidable may be satisfied with Sampson's *Concise History of English Literature*, a very remarkable abridgement of the larger work, which is also published by Macmillan.)

CARTER, John: *Binding Variants* (Constable, 1932).

——: *Detective Fiction* (Constable). (Note – This is an excellent groundwork and is not altogether superseded by Haycraft – see below. Carter's book is also a chapter in *New Paths* – see below.)

——: *Publisher's Cloth, 1820–1900* (Constable, 1935).

New Paths in Book-Collecting (Ed. by J. C.) (Scribner, 1934, $3.00).

See also Aldis above.

And G. Pollard: *An Enquiry into the Nature of Certain Nineteenth Century Pamphlets* (Scribner, 1934, $6.00).

CHAPMAN, R. W.: *Cancels* (Constable, 1932). See also under Courtney, below.

COLLINS, Arthur S.: *Authorship in the Days of Dr. Johnson* (Dutton, 1929, $5.00).

——: *The Profession of Letters* (Dutton, 1929, $5.00).

COURTNEY, William P. and SMITH, D. Nichol: *A Bibliography of Samuel Johnson* (Oxford, 1915, $2.50, illustrated edition, 1925). (Note – Much invaluable supplementary information is given in "Johnsonian Bibliography, a Supplement to Courtney" by R. W. Chapman and A. T. Hazen. This is printed in the *Proceedings of the Oxford Bibliographical Society*, v. 117–166.)

HARRIS, William J.: *The First Printed Translation into English of the Great Foreign Classics* (Dutton, 1909).

HARRISON, The Rev. Canon F.: *A Book About Books* (Murray, 1943).

HATTON, Thomas and CLEAVER, A. H.: *Bibliography of the Periodical Works of Charles Dickens* (Chapman and Hall, 1933). (Note – A book very much for the specialist only, but worth looking into if you find it on the shelves of a public library for the insight it gives into the methods of part publication in the nineteenth century.)

HAYCRAFT, Howard: *Murder for Pleasure* (Appleton-Century, $3.00).

HOPKINSON, Cecil: *Collecting Golf Books* (Constable, 1938).

KIDSON, F.: *British Music Publishers* (Hill, 1900).

LOWNDES, W. T.: *The Bibliographer's Manual* (Bohn, various editions). (Note – I have been taken to task for mentioning Lowndes in the same breath with the *Cambridge Bibliography of English Literature*, and it is, perhaps, advisable to add that Lowndes is, in the light of modern research, an unsatisfactory work with many shortcomings. He will be found on the shelves of most dealers in secondhand and rare books, however, and, although *C. B. E. L.* is a much mightier and more inclusive, as well as more reliable work, it is not worth, to the beginner, the $25.00 that it costs. My brief reference to it is possibly not worthy of the enormous labor that went into its preparation, and I may as well admit that it is a book that I should now find it hard to dispense with; nevertheless, it is not what it might have been and what so many hoped that it would be – a complete guide to English literature.)

McKERROW, Ronald B.: *An Introduction to Bibliography* (Clarendon Press).

MAIR, J.: *The Fourth Forger* (Macmillan, 1938, $2.75).

MEYERSTEIN, Edward W. H.: *A Life of Thomas Chatterton* (Ingpen and Grant). (Note – Once remaindered and still to be found at less than the published price, which should not deter the reader and student from acquiring a wonderfully documented and inclusive life of this short-lived poet.)

MUIR, P. H.: *Points*, first series (Smith, 1931, $7.50).

——: *Points*, second series (Bowker, 1934, $5.00).

MUMBY, Frank A.: *Publishing and Bookselling* (Bowker, 1931, $6.00).

NICHOLSON, H.: *The Development of Biography* (Hogarth Press).

ORCUTT, W. D.: *Master Makers of the Book* (Allen and Unwin, N.D.).

POLLARD, Alfred W.: *Old Picture Books* (Methuen, 1902).

——: *Books about Books* (6 vols., 1893), ed. by A. W. P.

——: *English Bookman's Library* (3 vols., 1900), ed. by A. W. P.

Pycroft, J.: *The Cricket Field*, edited by F. S. Ashley-Cooper (St. James's Press, 1922).

Ricci, S. de: *English Collectors of Books and Manuscripts (1530–1930)* (Cambridge University Press). (Note – This book entirely supersedes the books by Elton and Fletcher recommended on p. 114.)

Sadleir, Michael: *The Evolution of Publisher's Binding Styles* (Smith, 1930, $6.00).

Sharp, R. Farquharson: *A Dictionary of English Authors* (Redway, 1897).

Wheatley, H. B.: *The Prices of Books*

——: *The Booklover's Library*

——: Several vols. (ed. by H. B. W.), V. Y. (See pp. 113–14 for details.)

Index

INDEX

INDEX

INDEX

INDEX

INDEX

INDEX

INDEX

INDEX

PRINTER'S NOTE

The text of this book was set on the Linotype in Janson, a recutting made direct from the type cast from matrices made by Anton Janson some time between 1660 and 1687.

Of Janson's origin nothing is known. Some time between 1657 and 1668 Anton Janson, a punch-cutter and type-founder, bought from the Leipzig printer Johann Erich Hahn the type-foundry which had formerly been a part of the printing house of M. Friedrich Lankisch. Janson's types were first shown in a specimen sheet issued at Leipzig about 1675. Janson's successor, and perhaps his son-in-law, Johann Karl Edling, issued a specimen sheet of Janson types in 1689.

The book was composed, printed, and bound by The Plimpton Press, Norwood, Massachusetts. The printer's flower designs are free adaptations of arrangements by W. A. Dwiggins. The open-book ornament was drawn by Bruce Rogers and is used by permission of the Antioch Bookplate Company. We may extend this roster of typographical artists who have given delight to the world of fine books by stating that the Borzoi dog on the title page is from a border by T. M. Cleland and that the trademarks on the recto and verso of the binding are by W. A. Dwiggins and Rudolph Ruzicka, respectively.

J. H.